FULL OF BEANS

FULL OF BEANS
delicious beany
recipes to obsess over

Amelia Christie-Miller
Photography by Sam A Harris

KYLE BOOKS

First published in Great Britain in 2025
by Kyle Books, an imprint of Octopus
Publishing Group Ltd,
Carmelite House,
50 Victoria Embankment,
London EC4Y 0DZ
www.octopusbooks.co.uk
www.octopusbooksusa.com

An Hachette UK Company
www.hachette.co.uk

The authorized representative in the
EEA is Hachette Ireland, 8 Castlecourt
Centre, Dublin 15, D15 XTP3, Ireland
(email: info@hbgi.ie)

Text copyright ©
Amelia Christie-Miller 2025

Distributed in the US by Hachette Book
Group
1290 Avenue of the Americas,
4th and 5th Floors, New York,
NY 10104

Distributed in Canada by Canadian
Manda Group
664 Annette St., Toronto, Ontario,
Canada M6S 2C8

All rights reserved. No part of this work
may be reproduced or utilised in any
form or by any means, electronic or
mechanical, including photocopying,
recording or by any information storage
and retrieval system, without the prior
written permission of the publisher.

Amelia Christie-Miller asserts the moral
right to be identified as the author of this
work.

ISBN: 9781804192979

eISBN: 9781804192986

A CIP catalogue record for this book is
available from the British Library.

Printed and bound in China.

10 9 8 7 6 5 4 3 2 1

Publisher: Joanna Copestick
Project Editor: Sarah Reece
Copy Editor: Tara O'Sullivan
Art Director: Juliette Norsworthy
Designer: Nicky Collings
Photography: Sam A Harris
Food and props styling: Kitty Coles
Assistant Production Manager:
Allison Gonsalves

CONTENTS

Introduction	6
1 Butter Beans	12
2 Chickpeas	44
3 Borlotti Beans	68
4 Carlin Peas	90
5 Red Kidney Beans	114
6 White Beans	138
7 Black Beans	166
Thank Yous	188
Index	190
Glossary	192
Picture Credits	192

DIFFERENT JAR SIZES

You can find jarred beans in sizes of 570g, 660g or 700g (1lb 4½oz, 1lb 7oz or 1lb 9oz) – but don't panic! All our recipes work with a handful more or less of beans, this will just alter the number of servings – if using 700g (1lb 9oz) jars, allow one serving more than the recipe suggests.

KEY

 Vegetarian   Gluten free

 Vegan   Dairy free

INTRODUCTION

I'm aware I could be a little biased when it comes to this subject, but I do firmly believe we are living in the decade of beans.

For a while, we collectively shunned carbs, then we rediscovered them via sourdough topped with smashed avocado. We've been on journeys through low-fat, keto and fasting over the years, immersed in a cloud of protein powder, eating egg-white omelettes. But we're moving on – and beginning to see health more holistically. We're looking for something that ticks all the boxes: high in fibre, a source of protein and great for your gut, while actually being enjoyable and PLEASURABLE to eat. Well, guess what? It's beans.

We now know that health and food are impossible to separate, but the last 20 years have also taught us that sustainability and food are inextricably linked. The choices we make about what we put on our plates don't just affect us, they also ripple out to impact our environment. This next sentence comes with a trigger warning. We need to reduce our meat consumption. You know it, and I know it. One of the reasons we've found this undeniable truth so tough to digest is because all too often, the proposed replacement for a juicy roast chicken is a rubbery, ultra-processed alternative protein – not very appetising.

But there is good news. For people who love food, beans are the answer. In a world where we're increasingly feeling guilty about eating meat, beans are the exciting choice, the food we can rely on without compromising on one of life's greatest pleasures: eating. This book will show you how.

MY BEAN OBSESSION

Let me tell you where my bean obsession started. My career took me from private cheffing into working in the food-sustainability space. As someone who adores slow-roasted pork belly, delicate smoked fish and black pudding, this territory can be a challenging space in which to exist. On the one hand, I was living and breathing ALL delicious foods; on the other hand, I was learning about the impact that this delicious food – and our wider industrial food system – is having on our soils, climate and health. At first glance, it seemed that delicious food and a sustainable food system were incompatible – or, at the very least, required significant effort, like making blackened aubergine on a gas stove.

But then I discovered beans. Beans are high in protein, fibre and a host of minerals and vitamins. Beans are one of the most diverse food groups out there, and they're also nitrate-fixing plants, acting as natural fertilisers that support soil health and are fundamental in regenerative systems. Most importantly, beans are delicious, EXCITING and versatile. They make veg-centric meals so hearty and satisfying, you'll forget why you ever built your dinners around a joint of meat.

My bean obsession grew so potent that I ended up dedicating my life to a single mission – to make you equally obsessed with beans. Because – at least in the UK – we weren't starting on solid ground. Years of being seen as 'the poor man's meat' (aka peasant food) created a view of beans as a commodity: a food group solely traded on price. Nothing was being demanded from beans; they simply had to exist. This mentality led to quality being removed from each part of the cooking and sourcing process, leaving us with dull, dusty bullets we were taught to avoid. This was the first thing I wanted the Bold Bean Co. to sort out, by creating a range of beans so good you could treat them like Halkidiki olives, savouring them straight from the jar. By 2021, job one was complete and we launched a range of high-quality, expertly sourced and perfectly cooked beans into the UK market. Miraculously, in the years since, the British public have responded and welcomed these beans into their lives, and thanks to

this incredible community of bean fanatics – and my wonderful, bean-mad team – Bold Bean Co. beans are now stocked in most major British supermarkets.

The second thing we needed to resolve were the dishes in which beans were showing up – and there were very few! We wanted people to see beans being used in new, inventive ways – ways that looked so good it made their tummies rumble and their hands reach for the closest jar. Now, we have become known for our bean recipes – whether from our website, our Instagram posts or our first cookbook, *Bold Beans*. We make recipes that are celebratory, tempting and, of course, FULL OF BEANS.

FULL OF BEANS

Cookbooks are as much about inspiration as they are about teaching their readers certain tricks and skills, and this is something we've tried to bring into this book. We have several broader recipe templates, like the Five-Ingredient Traybakes on pages 110–13 and the Beanottos on pages 40–3, which you can simply follow or tweak to your own liking. Our mission is to arm you with the confidence to build beans into your daily refrigerator raids as well as your planned Sunday feasts, and that's exactly what these pages are here for.

We were completely blown away by how loved our first book was by our bean champs, and with this book, we've tried to really lean in to what worked in the last one. We've got dinner-party feasts and batch-cook beauties, as well as some speedy weeknight wonders. We've got spicy brunch plates (Smashed Chickpeas on Toast with Fried Egg + Pickled Cucumbers, page 54), Italian-inspired bowls (Borlotti alla Norma with Creamy Ricotta, page 72) and fragrant curries (Creamy Coconut + Tomato Curry, page 24). And, just as we did in the first book, we've included a range of guest recipes. But this time, they don't come from chefs, but from our very own bean champs. Over the years, we've come to realise that our Bold Bean community is full of the very best home cooks, and we are so excited to celebrate some of them in this book. We had so many contributions and were blown away by the quality.

We've got long-standing family recipes like Raina's Black Bean Makhani with Kachumber Salad (page 175), as well as modern veggie twists like Susie's Butter Bean Saganaki (page 19). We've tasted and tested all these contributing recipes, and they're truly some of my absolute favourites in this book. I know you will love them too.

In 2024, we launched our own version of the much-loved baked bean. We wanted to create baked beans made in the same way you would if you were making them from scratch in your kitchen. They're now being obsessed over for Sunday-night dinners and work-from-home lunches, but we've also heard that many of our customers are getting even more creative with them and using them as ingredients in exciting and indulgent recipes. So, of course, we've also included a section celebrating this – see pages 162–5.

After hearing the story of my desire to reduce my meat intake and promote a more sustainable diet, you'll probably be a bit surprised to see that we have recipes in this book that contain meat and fish. For me, this is key to bringing bean-haters on side. Food is incredibly emotive, and if you go from chicken Kievs and spag bol straight into a vegan bean terrine, you'll relapse and run to the closest McDonald's. To convert yourself (or someone you love) from a bean-hater to a bean-obsessive, you have to go easy. Beans make the most glorious partners for buttery melted anchovies, juicy browned sausages and freshly grilled fish, and these recipes are the gateway drug for the bean-sceptics. Then, before you know it, you're in the legume-inati and devouring recipes that are incidentally plant-based, but first and foremost are uncompromisingly delicious, satisfying and nutritious. In the words of a review for our first cookbook, you'll 'drift into eating vegetarian'. It won't be sudden or dramatic, but before you know it you'll look around and realise you're eating far less meat. I hate labels, but if I had to describe the way I eat it would be 'full of beans'. If you're eating this way, you'll be happier and healthier, and eating in a far more climate-friendly way.

- 60–70% water
- 20–25% carbs
- 6–9% protein
- 5–9% fibre
- < 1% fats

WHAT'S IN A BEAN?

If we wrote a chapter on each bean variety that exists, we'd need about twelve volumes. That's one of the most amazing things about beans – there are just so many of them!

We've concentrated on seven of the most popular beans for this book, and they're also the easiest to find in your local supermarket, whether you're using Bold Bean Co. beans or another brand.

CHICKPEAS
Highest fibre content

BUTTER BEANS
Richest source of potassium

WHITE BEANS (CANNELLINI)
Highest iron content

BORLOTTI BEANS
Rich in antioxidants

CARLIN PEAS
Highest protein content

BLACK BEANS
Highest polyphenol content

RED KIDNEY BEANS
Highest antioxidant activity

THE BEAN PLANOGRAM

For most of the recipes in this cookbook, substituting one bean for another will work – they all typically have a gentle flavour and soft texture. But there are better ways of substituting: by colour, and by size.

SUBSTITUTING BY COLOUR

We live in a visual world, and the food world is no exception. People eat with their eyes. That's why we've photographed almost all of the recipes in this book! When we create recipes, we think about the other ingredients and the balance of colours to make something look beautiful and tempting. White beans, being a blank canvas, work in almost any dish. We love pairing red beans with rich tomato-based recipes to double down on their ruby colour, while black beans hold up to darker sauces. If you want to keep a dish looking pretty, choose a substitute bean of a similar colour.

SUBSTITUTING BY SIZE

Think of this a bit like substituting pasta: the size and shape are what tend to matter most. Big beans are great for adding texture to a dish, so you may risk losing this if you substitute them with a smaller bean, which will probably cook faster and be softer. Smaller beans tend to offer a more uniform texture when used in certain recipes. And if the dish has lots of different elements, including dressing and herbs, you want each bite to be balanced – a larger bean will make it more of an effort to eat, as it would be trickier trying to guarantee every ingredient and enough dressing in every forkful.

A LEVEL PLAYING FIELD

In developing the recipes for this book, we used our own Bold Bean Co. beans — because we're very proud of our beans and how delicious they are! But that doesn't limit your ability to make knock-out bean-based meals even if you aren't using our beans. Here are some hacks to guarantee the same level of deliciousness.

THE JAR

While we can't guarantee other jarred bean brands will pay as much attention to soft skins and supple mouthfeel as us, the texture of jarred beans is, on the whole, going to be far more tender than canned varieties.

You can get the most out of jarred beans by using the WHOLE product, stock and all. Our own jars are filled with the best-tasting beans out there (thanks to our flavour-first sourcing) and their bean stock (the cooking liquor). We implore you not to throw this away — unless, of course, the recipe instructs you to drain and rinse the beans. Because we soak our beans and then discard this liquid before cooking them in fresh water, our bean stock doesn't contain any of the impurities that can cause gas in your gut. If you're using a different brand, check that they're not using additives, such as sulphites. If you do discard the stock, just add a small amount of veg stock to your recipe instead.

Some bean varieties release starches into the stock that can give it a gel-like consistency, but this is not something to be afraid of. It's actually something to get excited about, as these starches are packed with flavour and make MAGIC happen in Beanottos (see pages 40–3, 151 and 152) or stews. You might see a slightly darker-coloured stock at the top of some beans. This is a totally natural part of the oxidation process, so don't worry, the beans and stock will taste just as delicious!

THE CAN

Canned beans let the bean team down when delivering on flavour and texture. However, there is no denying that they're often super affordable and widely accessible so here is a nifty hack to use if you choose a can.

2 × 400g (14oz) cans beans (*opt for a variety most similar to the suggested jarred beans*)
1 tsp bicarbonate of soda
1 tsp salt (*if needed*)
¼ veg stock cube, *crumbled (if the recipe requires bean stock)*

1. Drain and rinse the beans in a sieve. Tip them into a saucepan. Fill the can with water and tip that in, half-fill it with water again and add this, along with the bicarbonate of soda. Add the salt if the beans don't already contain any. Bring to a boil, then reduce the heat to low and simmer for 15 minutes until the beans have softened. Drain and rinse.

2. Check the recipe you intend to use; does it require bean stock? If so, boil the kettle and, in a bowl, mash ½ tablespoon of the cooked beans with the stock cube. Pour 150ml (5fl oz/¼ pint) boiling water into the bowl and mix well so that the stock dissolves. Add the drained beans to the bowl of stock and combine. Or keep separate and use when needed.

CHEF + FOOD CAMPAIGNER

"I LOVE BEANS IN A BIG WAY. CREAMY, COMFORTING AND DELICIOUS, THEY'RE ONE OF THOSE INCREDIBLE INGREDIENTS THAT ARE ABLE TO TAKE ON FLAVOURS FROM ALL OVER THE WORLD. WHETHER YOU EAT THEM STRAIGHT UP, SERVE THEM ON TOAST, PAN-FRY THEM TILL THEY POP AND TOSS THEM THROUGH SALADS, SIMMER THEM IN STEWS OR SMASH THEM INTO DIPS, YOU'LL FIND THE POSSIBILITIES FOR DELICIOUSNESS ARE ENDLESS. PLUS, THEY'RE PLANT-BASED POWERHOUSES THAT ARE PACKED WITH FIBRE, A BRILLIANT SOURCE OF PROTEIN, AND LIVE HAPPILY IN YOUR STORE CUPBOARD FOR AGES. WHAT'S NOT TO LOVE?"

– Jamie Oliver

BUTTER BEANS

Big and buttery, rich and creamy, butter beans have real main-character energy.

TOMATO SOUP WITH CHEESY BUTTER BEANS

Feeds 4
Takes 45 minutes

Why is tomato soup so comforting? This one is boosted with butter beans in two ways: some are blitzed into the soup for silky smoothness, and some are roasted like croutons for a satisfying crunch. For the ultimate time-saving nostalgia, just blitz a shop-bought tomato soup with our butter beans and a kick of chilli, then pile on the croutons.

---

2 tbsp extra virgin olive oil, plus extra to serve

1 red or brown onion, roughly chopped

1 celery stalk, roughly chopped

3 garlic cloves finely chopped

1 red chilli / pinch of dried chilli flakes, finely chopped

1 tbsp tomato purée

2 × 400g (14oz) cans good-quality tomatoes

1 tbsp caster sugar, adjust to taste

30g (1oz) basil, leaves picked and stalks finely chopped

300ml (10fl oz/½ pint) milk

570g (1lb 4½oz) jarred butter beans, with their bean stock

50g (1¾oz) extra-mature Cheddar, grated

salt and pepper

1. Preheat the oven to 200°C/180°C fan/400°F/gas mark 6.

2. Heat 1 tablespoon of the olive oil in a large saucepan over a medium heat. Add the onion and celery, and season with a big pinch of salt and pepper. Cook for 15 minutes until soft, stirring occasionally, then chuck in the garlic and chilli and cook for a further 2 minutes.

3. Next, add the tomato purée and allow to cook out for a couple of minutes, before adding the tinned tomatoes, sugar, basil stalks, most of the basil leaves and the milk. Simmer away for 15–17 minutes.

4. Meanwhile, for the butter bean croutons, measure out half the butter beans using a slotted spoon so the bean stock is left behind. Rinse these beans, then pat them dry with paper towels. Tip them onto a baking tray and drizzle with the remaining 1 tablespoon of olive oil. Season with salt and pepper and pop into the oven for 25 minutes, adding the grated cheese for the final 5 minutes so it can go melted and crispy – make sure you focus the cheese gratings over the beans themselves!

5. Once the soup has been cooking for 15–17 minutes, pour in the remaining butter beans, along with all the bean stock, and cook for a further 2–3 minutes, just to warm the beans through.

6. When the soup has finished cooking, blend with a handheld blender until smooth. If you don't have a handheld blender, allow the soup to cool before transferring to a blender. Give the soup a taste and adjust the final seasoning if needed.

7. Serve the soup in deep bowls. Using a metal spatula, scrape the crispy, cheesy beans into crunchy bundles and place on top, along with the remaining basil leaves and a final drizzle of olive oil.

TOP TIP

Swap the milk for a full-fat plant-based milk if you prefer (oat milk is our favourite), and use either plant-based cheese or 1 tablespoon of nutritional yeast on the crispy beans.

CHEESY MARMITE BUTTER BEANS ON TOAST WITH PICKLED SHALLOTS

Feeds 4
Takes 20 minutes

Beans on toast meets cheese on toast, but with a twist. This version is all about umami Marmite, melty Cheddar and big, creamy butter beans – plus some tart pickled shallots to cut through it all. We want to see this on brunch menus ACROSS THE WORLD! Make sure that the bread is seriously toasty so it retains its crunch at every bite.

---

1 tbsp butter
1 tbsp Marmite, *adjust to taste*
570g (1lb 4½oz) jarred butter beans, *drained*
1 tbsp olive oil
4 large slices of sourdough
100g (3½oz) extra-mature Cheddar, *grated*
15g (½oz) fresh chives / 2 spring onions, *finely chopped (optional)*
salt and pepper

FOR THE PICKLED SHALLOTS
3 banana shallots, *thinly sliced*
2 tbsp red or white wine vinegar
1 tsp caster sugar

1. Ideally, you want to pickle the shallots at least an hour before serving. To do this, mix the shallots in a bowl or jar with the vinegar, sugar and a pinch of salt. Toss well, using your fingers to soften the shallots into the vinegar, and set aside to pickle while you prepare the beans. You can even do this a couple of days in advance and keep in the refrigerator until you need them.

2. Melt the butter in a large frying pan over a medium heat. Stir in the Marmite and mix until it melts into the butter. If you're a true Marmite lover, feel free to add more to suit your tastes.

3. Add the drained beans and stir to coat them in the Marmite-and-butter mixture. Cook for 2–3 minutes until the beans have warmed through.

4. While the beans are simmering, heat the olive oil in a separate frying pan over a medium-low heat. Add the sourdough slices and toast for 2–3 minutes on each side until golden and crispy. Alternatively, you could just pop them in the toaster.

5. Remove the beans from the heat and stir in half of the grated Cheddar. Season with plenty of cracked black pepper.

6. To assemble, generously spoon the cheesy Marmite butter beans over the toasted sourdough. Top with the remaining cheese, along with the quick-pickled shallots and the chives or spring onions for a kick of freshness. Serve immediately.

TOP TIP
Replace the butter and cheese with plant-based alternatives for a vegan-friendly version.

BUTTER BEAN SAGANAKI

Feeds 4
Takes 30 minutes

 SUSIE FLORY

Susie Flory has bold memories of eating prawn saganaki – a rich tomato sauce grilled with prawns and feta – on her first holiday to Greece. 'It was rich, creamy and paired BEAUTIFULLY with a glass of cold rosé.' Her version uses fresh tomatoes and our big, creamy butter beans, adding another layer of heavenly richness to this dish.

---

3 tbsp olive oil
1 onion, finely diced
2 fat garlic cloves, finely chopped
1 tbps tomato purée
500g (1lb 2oz) good-quality cherry tomatoes, halved
2 tsp smoked paprika
½ tsp dried chilli flakes
1 tsp dried oregano
zest of 2 lemons, juice of ½, plus wedges to serve
1 tsp honey
100ml (3½fl oz) rosé or white wine
570g (1lb 4½oz) jarred butter beans, with their bean stock
2 tbsp black olives, halved (optional)
150ml (5fl oz/¼ pint) veg stock (optional)
150g (5½oz) raw king prawns (optional)
200g (7oz) feta, crumbled
salt and pepper

TO SERVE
15g (½oz) parsley, roughly chopped
fresh crusty bread
rocket, dressed with lemon juice

1. Heat 2 tablespoons of the olive oil in a large, ovenproof frying pan over a medium heat. Add the onion and reduce the heat to low–medium. Cook for about 5 minutes, or until it starts to soften. Add the garlic, season and cook for a further minute until fragrant.

2. Increase the heat to medium–high and add the remaining olive oil, along with the tomato purée, tomatoes, smoked paprika, chilli flakes, oregano and lemon zest. Stir to combine, then add the honey and cook for 5–10 minutes, or until the tomatoes start to blister. If they start to stick, loosen them by adding a little water, a tablespoon at a time.

3. When the tomatoes are blistered and saucy, crush them a little, then add the wine, along with the beans and their stock, and the olives, if using. Stir to combine and bubble away over a medium heat for 5–6 minutes until the sauce reduces and thickens slightly. If it looks a little dry, add some or all of the veg stock.

4. Preheat the grill to medium–high.

5. Add the lemon juice to the tomato pan, along with the prawns, if using, then crumble over the feta. Slide under the grill for a few minutes until the feta has melted and charred in places, and the prawns, if using, have turned from grey to pink.

6. Divide between bowls, scatter over the parsley and serve with lemon wedges, a hunk of crusty bread and some fresh green leaves – we like rocket dressed with lemon juice.

> **TOP TIP**
> *If you are having people over, you can prepare this up to the end of step 3 earlier in the day, then slide it under the grill when ready to eat, for a speedy and impressive dinner.*

ROMESCO SAUCE WITH CRISPY BUTTER BEANS + CAPERS

Feeds 3
Takes 30 minutes

Romesco is a staple in Spanish cooking, and basically makes any dish feel like you're basking in the sun. We've kept ours pretty classic, but topped the smoky red pepper sauce with crisped-up butter beans and capers baked with fresh rosemary. Broccoli LOVES romesco, but if asparagus is in season, this will work just as well.

570g (1lb 4½oz) jarred butter beans, *drained and rinsed*

3 tbsp olive oil

2 rosemary sprigs, *leaves picked*

2 tbsp capers, *drained and dried on a paper towel*

salt and pepper

crusty bread or focaccia, *to serve (optional)*

FOR THE BROCCOLI

200g (7oz) Tenderstem broccoli

1 tbsp olive oil

zest of 1 lemon, *plus wedges to serve*

FOR THE ROMESCO SAUCE

100g (3½oz) blanched almonds

200g (7oz) roasted red peppers from a jar, *drained*

1 garlic clove

1–1½ tbsp sherry vinegar or red wine vinegar

1½ tsp sweet smoked paprika

½ tsp dried chilli flakes *(optional)*

3 tbsp extra virgin olive oil

1. Preheat the oven to 220°C/200°C fan/425°F/gas mark 7 and line a baking tray with baking paper.

2. Tip the rinsed beans onto a clean tea towel and pat them dry – you want them as dry as possible to become extra crispy. Tumble them onto the tray and toss well with the olive oil. Add the rosemary leaves and season. Roast for 20 minutes. Don't be alarmed if the butter beans start to crack – this helps achieve a good level of crispiness on the outside.

3. Pat the capers dry to remove any moisture, then toss them with the beans on the baking tray. Roast for a further 10–12 minutes until crispy.

4. Meanwhile, tumble the broccoli onto a second baking tray and drizzle with the olive oil. Season and roast for 10–15 minutes until charred.

5. While everything's in the oven, make the romesco sauce. Toast the almonds in a dry frying pan over a medium heat for 3–4 minutes until starting to turn golden and smelling toasty. Tip out and leave to cool.

6. In a food processor or blender, combine the cooled almonds, drained peppers, garlic, 1 tablespoon of the vinegar, the sweet smoked paprika, chilli flakes, if using, and a pinch of salt. Gradually add the olive oil and blend until the mixture is glossy, but still has some texture. Taste and adjust as needed, perhaps adding more vinegar for acidity or more chilli flakes for extra heat.

7. Once the butter beans and capers are crispy and golden, and the broccoli charred, remove from the oven and allow to cool slightly. Grate the lemon zest over the broccoli.

8. To serve, smooth the romesco sauce over a serving platter, then tumble over the crispy beans and capers. Serve with the broccoli and some lemon wedges, then dig in with crusty bread or focaccia.

TOP TIP

Once made, the romesco sauce will keep in the refrigerator for up to 5 days. Leftovers are unreal smooshed inside a sandwich with a bit of salty feta.

BEANY CAULIFLOWER CHEESE WITH SHERRY CHERRY TOMATOES

Feeds 4
Takes 45 minutes

This is classic comfort food with a beany twist. We LOVE this gratin – spiked with hot mustard and sharp Cheddar, featuring Parmesan-crusted cauliflower and butter beans for extra sauce, with tangy sherry-soaked cherry tomatoes to balance out the creaminess. If you're extra hungry, some leftover roasted chicken would be perfect here.

1 large head of cauliflower, cut into large florets
2 tbsp olive oil
40g (1½oz) Parmesan or vegetarian hard cheese, grated
40g (1½oz) butter
40g (1½oz) plain flour
400ml (14fl oz) milk
2 tsp English mustard
pinch of freshly grated or ground nutmeg
100g (3½oz) mature Cheddar, grated
570g (1lb 4½oz) jarred butter beans, with their bean stock
2 handfuls of breadcrumbs (we like fresh or panko)
30g (1oz) pumpkin or sunflower seeds
15g (½oz) parsley, roughly chopped (optional)
salt and pepper
mixed salad of your choice, to serve

FOR THE SHERRY CHERRY TOMATOES
500g (1lb 2oz) cherry tomatoes
2 tbsp olive oil
50ml (2fl oz) medium-dry sherry or vermouth

1. Preheat the oven to 220°C/200°C fan/425°F/gas mark 7.

2. Tip the cauliflower into a large, shallow baking dish and toss with the oil and a pinch of salt. Scatter with two-thirds of the Parmesan and roast for 25 minutes until crisp, golden and starting to char.

3. Meanwhile, make the cheese sauce. Melt the butter in a medium saucepan over a medium heat. Once melted, stir in the flour until you have a paste. Reduce the heat to a simmer and add the milk a splash at a time, stirring continuously until you have a smooth sauce that has thickened slightly.

4. Stir in the mustard and nutmeg along with about two-thirds of the grated Cheddar. Season to taste.

5. Tip the beans and their stock into the cheese sauce and mix well to combine. Remove the cauliflower from the oven and pour the beany, cheesy sauce over the top, ensuring the florets are fully coated. Scatter over the breadcrumbs and seeds, followed by the remaining Parmesan and Cheddar. Bake for 20–25 minutes until bubbling, crisp and golden.

6. Meanwhile, make the sherry cherry tomatoes. Tip the tomatoes into a second small roasting tin. Drizzle over the olive oil and season. Toss to coat the tomatoes well. Roast in the oven for 10 minutes, then add the sherry or vermouth and give the tray a shake to coat the tomatoes. Return to the oven and bake for an additional 10 minutes. The tomatoes should be soft but still hold their shape. Let them cool for a few minutes.

7. Serve the tomatoes with the cauliflower cheese bake, garnished with parsley for freshness, and some crisp salad leaves.

CREAMY COCONUT + TOMATO CURRY

Feeds 3
Takes 50 minutes

This coconut curry is golden, rich and warming, thanks to the earthy turmeric and slow-roasted tomatoes, and is also super simple to make. Whizzing up some of the butter beans makes it ultra creamy and velvety – we would definitely recommend. Finish with the zingy coriander salsa to lift the flavours and add freshness.

300g (10½oz) large vine tomatoes, *halved*

2 tsp cumin seeds

2 tbsp neutral oil, *such as sunflower or rapeseed oil*

100g (3½oz) cherry tomatoes

1 onion, *sliced*

2 garlic cloves, *crushed or finely chopped*

thumb-sized piece of fresh ginger, *peeled and grated*

1 red chilli, *deseeded and sliced*

1 tsp ground turmeric

1 tsp garam masala

400ml (14fl oz) can full-fat coconut milk / 160ml (5½fl oz) coconut cream

100g (3½oz) spinach

570g (1lb 4½oz) jarred butter beans, *with their bean stock*

salt

FOR THE CORIANDER SALSA

20g (¾oz) coriander, *very finely chopped*

juice of 2 limes

1 tbsp olive oil

pinch of caster sugar

TO SERVE (OPTIONAL)

nigella seeds

cooked basmati rice

1. Preheat the oven to 200°C/180°C fan/400°F/gas mark 6.

2. Put the large tomatoes on a large oven tray and sprinkle with half of the cumin seeds, a pinch of salt and 1 tablespoon of the oil. Roast for an initial 10 minutes, then tip in the cherry tomatoes and roast for a further 20 minutes, until they are all soft and starting to caramelise.

3. Meanwhile, heat the remaining oil in a saucepan over a medium heat. Add the onion and cook for about 10 minutes until starting to soften. Add the garlic, ginger and chilli, and cook for a further 2 minutes until fragrant.

4. Stir in the turmeric, garam masala, remaining cumin seeds and a pinch of salt. Cook out the spices for 2–3 minutes until they smell fragrant, then add the coconut milk or cream to the pan, along with any bean stock that's easy to drain from the jar. Blend with a handheld blender until smooth. (If you're using coconut milk, you may want to add some of the butter beans here to thicken the sauce naturally.) Once blended, add the spinach and butter beans, with the rest of their bean stock. Simmer gently for 10–12 minutes.

5. In a small bowl, mix the coriander with the two-thirds of the lime juice. Stir in the olive oil and sugar, and mix well to form a salsa.

6. Once the tomatoes are cooked, remove from the oven and add them to the curry, along with any juices. Add the rest of the lime juice and stir to combine.

7. Spoon the curry into bowls. Drizzle with the coriander salsa and sprinkle with nigella seeds, if you like. Serve with rice for an extra-hearty meal.

SAUSAGE + BUTTER BEAN STEW

Feeds 2–3
Takes 40 minutes

A dish is only as good as the ingredients you cook with – and this rule is particularly important here. This is essentially a two-hero ingredient, one-pot dish, with sausages and beans taking centre stage. The stew is saucy and unctuous, its richness lifted by a bright basil salsa. The sausages can be squeezed out of their skins if you want a different texture.

---

1 tbsp olive oil
6 sausages of your choice
1 onion, finely diced
1 carrot or celery stalk, finely diced
1 red pepper, roughly chopped
3 garlic cloves, finely chopped
1 tbsp tomato purée
1 tsp dried or fresh rosemary, finely chopped
1 teaspoon dried or fresh thyme, finely chopped
400g (14oz) can plum tomatoes
1 tbsp Worcestershire sauce or Henderson's Relish
1 tsp soft light brown or caster sugar
2 bay leaves (optional)
1 beef or veg stock cube
570g (1lb 4½oz) jarred butter beans, with their bean stock
salt and pepper

FOR THE BASIL SALSA VERDE

handful of parsley, roughly chopped
small bunch of basil, roughly chopped
1 tsp Dijon mustard
3 tbsp extra virgin olive oil
1 tbsp capers, plus a splash of their juice
zest and juice of ½ lemon

1. Heat the olive oil in a large saucepan or casserole dish over a medium heat. Add the sausages (whole or squeezed out of their skins into meatball-sized pieces) and cook for 8–10 minutes (for whole) or 7–8 minutes (if in pieces) until browned. Remove from the pan using tongs and set aside on a plate.

2. To the same pan, add the onion, carrot or celery and red pepper, and cook for 8–10 minutes in the sausage fat, stirring regularly until softened (add a splash more oil if necessary). Add the garlic, tomato purée, rosemary and thyme, and cook for about 2 minutes until fragrant.

3. Add the tomatoes, then fill the can about a third full of water, give it a swirl, and throw that in too. Stir in the Worcestershire sauce or Henderson's relish, sugar and bay leaves, if using, and crumble in the stock cube.

4. Return the sausages to the pan. Stir to combine, then simmer on a low heat for 3–4 minutes, before adding the butter beans with their bean stock. Simmer for a further 7–8 minutes to allow the flavours to infuse and the sauce to thicken slightly.

5. Meanwhile, mix all of the ingredients for the basil salsa verde in a small bowl and season to taste.

6. Taste the stew and season if necessary. Ladle into bowls, top with the salsa verde, and enjoy!

> **TOP TIP**
> This is a great one for batch cooking. Simply double up on the stew, then freeze in individual portions for a speedy and comforting meal whenever you need one.

CREAMY LEEK, MUSHROOM + BUTTER BEAN PIE

Feeds 4–6
Takes 1 hour 20 minutes

You just can't beat a pie. There is something about crispy, buttery pastry and a comforting creamy filling that really hits the spot. Add butter beans and you've got yourself an indulgent supper that is just as wonderful veggie or with smoky pancetta. If you're leaving out the pancetta, taste test as you go, adding a little more salt if needed.

---

1 tsp olive oil (optional)
100g (3½oz) pancetta (optional)
20g (¾oz) butter
2 leeks, roughly chopped
150g (5½oz) chestnut or button mushrooms, roughly sliced
3 garlic cloves, finely chopped
2–3 thyme sprigs, leaves stripped
1 tbsp wholegrain or Dijon mustard
1 tbsp plain flour
150ml (5fl oz/¼ pint) white wine
250–350ml (9–12fl oz) chicken or veg stock
570g (1lb 4½oz) jarred butter beans, drained
100ml (3½fl oz) double cream
1 egg
240g (8½oz) ready-rolled puff pastry
salt and pepper

TO SERVE
buttered peas
cheesy mashed potato (optional)

1. Preheat the oven to 180°C/160°C fan/350°F/gas mark 4.

2. If you're using pancetta, heat the olive oil in a large frying pan over a medium heat. Add the pancetta and cook for 6–8 minutes until crisp. Remove from the pan with a slotted spoon and set aside.

3. To the same pan, add the butter, leeks and mushrooms. Season and cook for 10–12 minutes until softened, then add the garlic and thyme leaves. Cook for a couple of minutes, then add the mustard and flour and cook for a few minutes more, stirring all the while.

4. Pour in the white wine and let it bubble away for a few minutes before gradually adding 250ml (9fl oz) of the stock, stirring constantly. Add the butter beans, cream and reserved pancetta, if using. Season well with black pepper and cook for 10 minutes. If it starts to look a little dry, add a splash more stock. Once it's ready, pour the pie filling into a large pie dish and allow to cool completely.

5. Whisk the egg in a small bowl and use some of it to brush the top edges of the pie dish. Take the pastry and lay it over the pie filling – you may need to roll out the pastry slightly first, depending on the shape of your pie dish – then cut away any loose edges and crimp with a fork. If you're feeling fancy, you can use any excess pastry to decorate the top. Brush the pastry with the remaining egg and season with salt. Bake for 35–40 minutes until the pastry is puffed up and deeply golden.

6. Leave the pie to rest for a few minutes, then serve in the middle of the table for people to help themselves, along with buttered peas, and maybe some cheesy mashed potato.

TOP TIP
The pie filling can be prepared the day before and kept in the refrigerator until you are ready to assemble the pie and bake.

LEMONY RICOTTA + BUTTER BEAN DIP WITH SMASHED CRISPY POTATOES

Feeds 4 as a dip or starter
Takes 35 minutes

Lemon, ricotta and butter beans are a classic combination. The creaminess of the beans complements the ricotta, while the lemon brightens everything and brings it all to life. Here, we've transformed this combo into a dip that's so good you'll be wanting to eat it with everything – especially these crispy fennel-spiked potatoes!

570g (1lb 4½oz) jarred butter beans, *drained*
100g (3½oz) ricotta
zest of 1½ lemons, juice of 1
1 garlic clove, *peeled*
small handful of parsley, *finely chopped*
extra virgin olive oil, *for drizzling*
salt and pepper

FOR THE CRISPY POTATOES
500g (1lb 2oz) new potatoes
2 tbsp olive oil
1 tsp fennel seeds

1. Preheat the oven to 220°C/200°C fan/425°F/gas mark 7.

2. Fill a large pot with salted water and bring to the boil. Add the new potatoes and cook for 15 minutes until tender.

3. Meanwhile, prepare the dip. In a blender or food processor, combine the drained beans, ricotta, lemon zest and juice, and garlic. Blitz until completely smooth, then season to taste. Transfer the dip to a bowl and stir in the parsley. Set aside.

4. Once cooked, drain the potatoes and leave to steam dry for a few minutes. Tumble the potatoes onto a baking tray and, using the back of a fork or a potato masher, gently smash them. Drizzle the smashed potatoes with the olive oil, sprinkle with the fennel seeds, and season.

5. Roast the potatoes for 15–20 minutes, or until golden and crispy.

6. Serve the dip in a bowl, drizzled with a bit of extra virgin olive oil, with the warm, crispy smashed potatoes on the side for dipping.

TOP TIP
Once the dip is made, it will keep for 3 days in the refrigerator, and is delicious in place of hummus in sandwiches – we particularly like it with roasted broccoli on focaccia.

BUTTER BEAN TAGINE FEAST WITH OLIVE + LEMON SALSA

Feeds 6
Takes 45 minutes

Feast your eyes on this. Creamy butter beans are gently simmered in a fragrant, spiced tagine, absorbing all the deep, aromatic flavours of cumin, coriander and cinnamon. Served alongside fluffy, herby bulgur wheat and a tangy olive-and-lemon salsa, it's easy to prep in advance and is guaranteed to impress at a dinner party or Sunday lunch.

2 tbsp extra virgin olive oil
1 large onion, *finely chopped*
2 carrots, *finely chopped*
3 fat garlic cloves, *finely chopped*
1½ tbsp ras el hanout
2 tsp paprika
2 tsp ground cumin
2 tsp ground cinnamon
2 tsp honey or maple syrup
2 tbsp rose harissa paste
2 × 570g (1lb 4½oz) jarred butter beans, *with their bean stock*
150ml (5fl oz/¼ pint) veg stock
400g (14oz) can chopped tomatoes
60g (2¼oz) dried apricots, raisins or sultanas *(optional)*
salt and pepper

FOR THE TABBOULEH
150g (5½oz) bulgur wheat or quinoa
15g (½oz) each mint, parsley and coriander, *finely chopped*
100g (3½oz) pomegranate seeds
juice of 1 lemon
2 tbsp extra virgin olive oil

FOR THE SALSA
50g (1¾oz) flaked almonds or sunflower or pumpkin seeds
100g (3½oz) pitted green olives, *sliced*
2 preserved lemons, *quartered, flesh removed and rind finely chopped*
15g (½oz) parsley, *finely chopped*
2 tbsp extra virgin olive oil

1. Heat the olive oil in a large casserole pan over a medium–high heat. Add the onion, carrots and a pinch of salt, and cook for 10 minutes, stirring regularly, until softened. Add the garlic and cook for another minute, then stir in the ras el hanout, paprika, cumin, cinnamon, honey or maple syrup and harissa paste. Cook for 3 minutes, mixing well.

2. Pour the butter beans and their bean stock into the pan, along with the veg stock and chopped tomatoes. Fill the tomato can about a third full of water, give it a swirl, and throw that in too. Add the apricots, raisins or sultanas, if using, then bring to a simmer and cook for 22–25 minutes so that the flavours mingle and the sauce thickens and reduces slightly.

3. Meanwhile, prepare the tabbouleh. Cook the bulgur wheat or quinoa according to the packet instructions. Drain and leave to cool.

4. Tip the cooled bulgur or quinoa into a large bowl and add the remaining tabbouleh ingredients. Season with a pinch of salt and mix well to combine. Taste and add more seasoning or lemon juice to your liking.

5. To make the salsa, toast the almonds or seeds in a small dry frying pan over a medium heat for a couple of minutes until golden, tossing regularly. Tip into a bowl and mix with the remaining salsa ingredients.

6. Scatter some of the salsa over the tagine, reserving some for the table, and place the pan in the centre of the table, alongside the tabbouleh, and perhaps some yoghurt and flatbreads, if you like. Let everyone tuck in, helping themselves to sides as they go!

TOP TIP
If you don't have ras el hanout, make your own by combining 1 teaspoon each of ground cumin, ground cinnamon, paprika and ground ginger.

ZA'ATAR BUTTER BEAN SALAD WITH CREAMY BUTTER BEAN DIP

Feeds 2 as a main or 4 as a side
Takes 20 minutes

This is butter beans two ways: za'atar spiced and left whole, and a creamy, smooth dip inspired by hummus. Za'atar is a Middle Eastern spice blend that's equal parts earthy, tangy, nutty and citrussy, pairing well with the bitter parsley, peppery radishes and juicy pomegranate seeds used here.

100g (3½oz) green beans

1 tbsp za'atar spice blend, *plus extra to serve*

½ × 570g (1lb 4½oz) jarred butter beans, *with their bean stock*

1 large cucumber, halved lengthways, *deseeded and finely chopped*

8 radishes, *finely sliced*

40g (1½oz) pomegranate seeds

30g (1oz) mixed herbs (mint, basil, parsley and/or dill), *leaves roughly chopped*

1 tbsp lemon juice

1 tbsp extra virgin olive oil, *plus extra to serve*

salt and pepper

FOR THE BUTTER BEAN DIP
½ × 570g (1lb 4½oz) jarred butter beans, *with their bean stock*

2 tbsp tahini

juice of 1 lemon

1 garlic clove, *crushed*

2 tbsp extra virgin olive oil

TO SERVE (OPTIONAL)
pomegranate molasses
warm flatbreads or pittas

1. First, prepare the butter bean dip. Add all the ingredients to a blender and blitz until combined. Check for consistency, adding 1–2 tablespoons of cold water to loosen if necessary. You want it to be fairly thick but smooth. Adjust the seasoning to taste, then set aside. (This can be made up to 3 days in advance and stored in the refrigerator until needed – make sure you bring the dip up to room temperature before serving though.)

2. Cook the green beans in a pan of salted boiling water for 3–4 minutes until just cooked – you want them to still have some bite. Drain and refresh under cold water – even better if you can make it icy. Set aside.

3. This next step is optional, but does help to bring out more flavour. Toast the za'atar in a dry frying pan over a low–medium heat for 1–2 minutes until it turns golden brown and is smelling nutty.

4. Tip the butter beans into a large mixing bowl, along with the za'atar, cucumber, radishes, green beans, pomegranate seeds and fresh herbs. Drizzle with the lemon juice and olive oil and toss gently to coat. Season to taste.

5. To assemble, spread the bean dip onto a large serving platter and tumble over the bean salad. Sprinkle extra za'atar on top and finish with a drizzle of olive oil and additional pomegranate seeds. Serve immediately. If you like, you can drizzle over some pomegranate molasses and put warm flatbreads or pittas on the table for scooping.

TOP TIP
If you're extra hungry, some halloumi, fried until golden, would be a stunning addition to this dish.

CARAMELISED FENNEL, SUN-DRIED TOMATO + BUTTER BEAN SALAD

Feeds 3 as a main, 4 as a side
Takes 25 minutes

This salad will transport you to the Mediterranean, because a salad full of sun-dried tomatoes, briny capers and salty Parmesan always tastes like a holiday in the sun. Caramelising the fennel mellows and sweetens its aniseed flavour. WARNING: This dish will probably tempt you into booking a flight to warmer shores.

---

4 tbsp extra virgin olive oil

2 large fennel bulbs, sliced into wedges

50g (1¾oz) pine nuts or sunflower seeds

570g (1lb 4½oz) jarred butter beans, drained

100g (3½oz) sun-dried tomatoes, each chopped into thirds

2 tbsp capers / a handful of kalamata olives, chopped

100g (3½oz) rocket

juice of 1 lemon

50g (1¾oz) pecorino or Parmesan or vegetarian hard cheese

salt

1. Heat 2 tablespoons of the olive oil in a large frying pan over a medium heat. Add the fennel and a good pinch of salt and fry for 15–20 minutes, turning regularly, until golden and soft. For the last 5 minutes of cooking, reduce the heat slightly, add 2 tablespoons of water and cover the pan with a lid to help soften the fennel.

2. Meanwhile, toast the pine nuts or sunflower seeds in a separate dry frying pan over a low heat for 2–3 minutes until golden.

3. Combine the drained beans, sun-dried tomatoes, capers or olives, rocket and lemon juice in a large mixing bowl with the remaining olive oil. Toss well to combine.

4. Tip this mixture onto a serving platter and arrange the fennel wedges on top. Shave over the pecorino or Parmesan using a veg peeler, and scatter over the nuts or seeds. Serve immediately.

BROWN BUTTER + CAPER BEANS WITH RAW COURGETTE SALAD

Feeds 2–3
Takes 20 minutes

The smell of briny capers mingling with nutty brown butter is unbelievably good, but throw creamy butter beans into the mix and you'll have landed in heaven. The richness of the buttery beans is cut through by the herby, lemony raw courgettes, which can be marinated a couple of hours ahead. If in season, try asparagus for a great alternative!

50g (1¾oz) pumpkin seeds or pine nuts
50g (1¾oz) butter
1–2 garlic cloves, *thinly sliced*
3 tbsp capers, *drained and roughly chopped*
570g (1lb 4½oz) jarred butter beans, *drained and rinsed*
zest and juice of 1 lemon
salt and pepper

FOR THE RAW COURGETTE SALAD
2 courgettes, *thinly sliced into ribbons using a peeler*
1 tbsp olive oil
2 tbsp lemon juice
10g (¼oz) mint, *roughly chopped*
10g (¼oz) basil, *roughly chopped*
pinch of dried chilli flakes *(optional)*

TO SERVE (OPTIONAL)
pecorino or vegetarian hard cheese
toasted soda bread

1. The raw courgette salad can be made a couple of hours ahead of time to allow the flavours to mellow. To prepare the salad, combine all the ingredients in a large bowl. Season with a good pinch of salt and toss well to coat.

2. When you're ready to prepare the rest of the meal, toast the pumpkin seeds (or pine nuts) in a large, dry frying pan over a medium heat for 2–3 minutes until golden, then tip into a bowl and set aside.

3. In the same large pan, melt the butter over a medium–low heat. Cook for about 5 minutes, swirling occasionally, until the butter turns a deep golden brown and smells nutty. Add the garlic and capers to the brown butter, and cook for another minute until fragrant.

4. Reduce the heat right down and tip the drained beans into the pan, along with a pinch of salt, making sure to shake off any excess water from the sieve first. Stir gently to coat them in the brown butter and caper mixture. Warm through for 3–4 minutes, then pour the lemon juice over the beans and season to taste.

5. Serve the beans alongside the raw courgette salad, sprinkled with the toasted seeds or nuts. Sprinkle over the lemon zest for extra brightness, and finish with a few shavings of pecorino, if you like. Serve as it is for a light summer lunch or dinner, or with toasted soda bread for a heartier meal.

THE BEANOTTO

THE BASE

The beanotto is a risotto-inspired belter of a dish, and a total game-changer.

Instead of rice, we use BEANS. Starchy white beans, to be specific, as they absorb all the delicious flavours and melt in the mouth. Beanottos have all the indulgence of a regular risotto, are made in a fraction of the time, and are packed with fibre and protein. Simply begin with the Beanotto Base below, then proceed with your chosen recipe.

1. Heat 1 tablespoon of olive oil (with a knob of butter, if you have it) in a large pan over a low heat.

2. Add 1 finely chopped onion and 2 finely chopped garlic cloves, along with a pinch of salt.

3. Cook gently for 10–15 minutes until softened but not coloured.

4. Increase the heat to medium-high. Add 250ml (9fl oz) dry white wine.

5. Let it bubble away until only a little is left in the onion mixture. Your beanotto base is ready.

BEETROOT + GOATS' CHEESE

250g (9oz) vacuum-packed cooked beetroots with their juice, diced into 2cm (¾in) chunks

1 tbsp fresh thyme leaves, roughly chopped

570g (1lb 4½oz) jarred white beans, with their bean stock

150g (5½oz) soft goats' cheese, chopped or crumbled

handful of beetroot crisps

1. Tip half of the beetroots into a blender with a splash of their juice and blitz into a smooth purée. Add this and the chopped beetroots to the beanotto base, along with the thyme.

2. Add the white beans and their stock to the pan and stir to combine. Simmer for 3–4 minutes to allow the flavours to mingle. Season to taste.

3. Divide into bowls and top with the goats' cheese and the beetroot crisps. Finish with toasted nuts, if you like, and a squeeze of lemon.

Works with **White beans**

CREAMY COURGETTE

2 courgettes, *1 sliced into 5mm (¼in) rounds, 1 coarsely grated*

2 tsp fennel seeds *(optional)*

2 garlic cloves, *roughly chopped*

zest of ½ lemon, juice of 1

570g (1lb 4½oz) jarred white beans, *with their bean stock*

1 heaped tbsp crème fraîche

25g (1oz) Parmesan or vegetarian hard cheese, *plus extra to serve*

handful of parsley, *roughly chopped*

handful of fresh basil leaves, *torn*

handful of pine nuts, *toasted*

1. Add both the sliced and grated courgettes to the beanotto base, along with a pinch of salt and the fennel seeds, if using. Cook for 7–8 minutes until starting to soften and colour.

2. Add the garlic and lemon zest and cook for 2 minutes.

3. At this point, add your white beans and their stock to the pan and let it bubble away for 2 minutes.

4. Reduce the heat to low. Stir in the crème fraîche, Parmesan and herbs, then season and add lemon juice to taste. Mix everything well to combine and cook on a low heat for a further minute.

5. Serve into bowls and top with a little more Parmesan. Finish with toasted pine nuts and a drizzle of olive oil.

THE BEANOTTO continued

BUTTERNUT SQUASH + SAGE

1 butternut squash, cut into chunks

3 tbsp olive oil

570g (1lb 4½oz) jarred white beans, with their bean stock

1 tsp grated or ground nutmeg

small bunch of sage, leaves picked, half roughly chopped, half left whole

grated Parmesan or vegetarian hard cheese (optional)

toasted pine nuts (optional)

1. Preheat the oven to 200°C (180°C fan/400°F/gas mark 6). Scatter the squash chunks onto a baking tray, drizzle with 1 tablespoon of the oil, season, toss to coat, then roast for 35–40 minutes until soft and caramelised. Transfer half the squash chunks to a blender and blitz into a purée. Set aside.

2. Add the jar of white beans and their stock to the beanotto base, along with the nutmeg and sage. Let it cook for a few minutes, then add the purée, stir, then add the squash chunks. Taste and season as needed.

3. Stir over a low heat for 5 minutes until warmed through and looking silky.

4. Meanwhile, heat the remaining olive oil in a small frying pan over a medium heat, and gently fry the whole sage leaves, working in batches, for about 30 seconds until crisp. Set aside on a plate lined with paper towels.

5. When your beanotto is warmed through, finish with the crispy sage leaves, along with some grated Parmesan and toasted pine nuts, if you like.

TOP TIP
To finish any of the beanottos described here, fold through a small knob of butter or 1 tablespoon of extra virgin olive oil, along with 1 tablespoon of grated Parmesan or vegetarian hard cheese before serving.

Works with **White beans**

CHORIZO + CHERRY TOMATO

75g (2¾oz) cooking chorizo, diced

1 large rosemary sprig, *leaves picked and roughly chopped*

zest of ½ lemon

1 tsp smoked paprika

½–1 tsp dried chilli flakes

400g (14oz) can cherry tomatoes, drained

570g (1lb 4½oz) jarred white beans, with their bean stock

15g (½oz) parsley, *roughly chopped*

1. Add the cooking chorizo, rosemary leaves, lemon zest, smoked paprika, chilli flakes and cherry tomatoes to the beanotto base and cook for 2–3 minutes.

2. Add your jar of white beans and their stock to the pan and warm through. Taste and adjust the seasoning to your liking.

3. Cook for a further 4–5 minutes until piping hot, then add most of the parsley and stir through.

4. Serve into bowls and top with the remaining parsley.

PSYCHOLOGIST

"EAT MORE BEANS. BELIEVE ME, THEY'RE THE ANSWER TO MOST OF YOUR – AND THE PLANET'S – MOST PRESSING PROBLEMS. YOU CAN'T HAVE GOOD MENTAL HEALTH WITHOUT A WELL-FUNCTIONING BRAIN, AND YOU CAN'T HAVE A WELL-FUNCTIONING BRAIN WITHOUT GOOD NUTRITION."

– Kimberley Wilson

CHICKPEAS

Chickpeas bring a creamy nuttiness to the table and have serious superfood status, so they're good for your gut as well as your tastebuds.

SILKY ROASTED GARLIC HUMMUS + COURGETTE BOWL

Feeds 4 as a dip
Takes 40 minutes

This roasted garlic hummus is soft, silky and decadent – a certified crowd-pleaser for your next picnic in the park or potluck supper. Roasting the garlic leaves it sweet, earthy and caramelised, which is obviously delicious alone, but even better when whizzed up with tahini. Enjoy with crusty bread to dip into that chickpea goodness.

½ **garlic bulb (5–6 cloves)**
3 large courgettes, sliced into 1cm (½in) rounds
5 tbsp extra virgin olive oil
20g (¾oz) pine nuts or pumpkin seeds
3 tbsp tahini
570g (1lb 4½oz) jarred chickpeas, with their bean stock
zest and juice of 1 lemon
large pinch of za'atar / a mixture of sumac and dried chilli flakes
salt

TO SERVE
crudités
crusty bread or warm pittas

1. Preheat the oven to 180°C/160°C fan/350°F/gas mark 4.

2. Wrap the garlic cloves (still in their skins) in foil and place on a baking tray. Roast for 30 minutes until soft and tender.

3. Line a large baking tray with baking paper and arrange the courgette rounds across it in a single layer. Drizzle with 2 tablespoons of the olive oil and roast for 25–30 minutes until golden and caramelised, turning halfway so that they roast evenly.

4. Meanwhile, toast the pine nuts or pumpkin seeds in a separate small roasting tin in the oven for 3–5 minutes until evenly golden. Set aside.

5. Remove the garlic from the oven and allow to cool slightly.

6. To make the hummus, put the tahini, the chickpeas and their bean stock and the remaining 3 tablespoons olive oil into a blender. Add half of the lemon juice and a pinch of salt. Carefully squeeze the garlic cloves out of their skins straight into the blender, then blend until super smooth and silky. Check for seasoning and acidity, adding more salt and lemon juice if desired.

7. Spoon the hummus onto a large plate or bowl, then tumble the courgette slices over the top. Sprinkle over the pine nuts or pumpkin seeds, lemon zest and za'atar or sumac and chilli flakes before digging in with your choice of crudités and bread.

8. Once made, the hummus will keep happily in the refrigerator for up to 5 days, making it the perfect snack/addition to your working lunch.

PICKLED CUCUMBER WITH CHICKPEAS + STICKY RICE

Feeds 2
Takes 30 minutes

V D

SAMANTHA LEUNG

Inspired by Samantha Leung's nostalgia for homecooked food from Hong Kong, this is a beany twist on a tongue-tingling classic. She says: 'I would always find myself calling my mom, asking her for recipes whenever I was craving something homecooked.' Make a big batch of these cucumbers and keep them in the refrigerator for adding zing to a dish.

---

1 cucumber, *roughly cut into bite-sized chunks*

½ tsp flaky sea salt

3 tbsp rice wine vinegar

handful of coriander, *finely chopped, some leaves reserved for garnish*

1 tsp caster sugar

½ tsp ground white or black pepper

150g (5½oz) sushi or sticky rice

2 tbsp sesame oil

1 fat garlic clove, *grated*

thumb-sized piece of fresh ginger, *grated*

570g (1lb 4½oz) jarred chickpeas, *drained, rinsed, and patted dry with a paper towel*

1 tsp honey or maple syrup

2 tsp crispy chilli oil, *adjust to taste, plus extra to serve*

salt

TO SERVE

1 tbsp toasted sesame seeds

sriracha mayo *(optional)*

1. Put the cucumber chunks in a bowl with the flaky sea salt and toss to coat. Leave to sit for 5–10 minutes until they start releasing water. Drain the liquid, leaving just the cucumbers.

2. Add the vinegar, chopped coriander, sugar and pepper to the cucumber. Toss well to combine, then set aside to marinate in the flavours.

3. Rinse the rice in a sieve under cold water for 30 seconds, then set aside to drain fully.

4. Tip the drained rice into a medium saucepan for which you have a lid, then add 200ml (7fl oz/⅓ pint) water and a generous pinch of salt. Place the pan over a high heat and bring almost to the boil (if it fully boils, the rice will stick to the pot). Just before the water reaches boiling point, reduce the heat to low until very gently bubbling and cook for 15 minutes with the lid on (this will ensure perfectly fluffy rice). After 15 minutes, remove the pot from the heat and keep covered for a further 10 minutes while you prepare the chickpeas.

5. Heat the sesame oil in a frying pan over a medium heat. Add the garlic and ginger, along with the chickpeas and honey. Fry for 5–6 minutes until slightly crispy, then add the crispy chilli oil and fry for a few minutes more. You may want to put a lid on in case the chickpeas pop in the pan! If they do start popping, just reduce the heat a little. Once crispy, take off the heat and leave to cool.

6. Scoop the sticky rice into bowls, plate up the pickled cucumbers on the side and, once slightly cooled, add the crispy chickpeas on top.

7. Serve with a good drizzle of chilli oil (or sriracha mayo if you fancy something creamier), topped with a sprinkle of sesame seeds and some picked coriander leaves.

CHUNKY FETA YOGHURT, SUN-RIPENED TOMATOES + CHICKPEAS WITH FOCACCIA

Feeds 3–4 as a starter or sharing plate
Takes 15 minutes

A super-easy number for when you're entertaining. There's zero fuss or faff here, just lots of good-quality ingredients thrown together. Toasting the pine nuts and the focaccia is the only cooking involved. The result is garlicky, zesty and creamy – an incredibly simple treat that you'll be able to knock out 15 minutes before everyone arrives.

50g (1¾oz) pine nuts

570g (1lb 4½oz) jarred chickpeas, *drained*

130g (4½oz) semi-dried tomatoes, *roughly chopped*

2 fat garlic cloves, *1 grated and 1 kept whole*

pinch of dried chilli flakes or Aleppo pepper flakes

3 tbsp extra virgin olive oil, *plus extra to serve*

1 tsp sherry vinegar or red wine vinegar *(optional, but really helps lift the flavour of the basil)*

½ small bunch basil

250g (9oz) focaccia, *cut into 8 slices*

200g (7oz) thick, full-fat Greek yoghurt

200g (7oz) feta

zest of 1 lemon, juice of ½

salt and pepper

1. Toast the pine nuts in a dry frying pan over a low–medium heat for 2–3 minutes until golden all over.

2. Preheat the grill to medium.

3. Tumble the chickpeas, semi-dried tomatoes, garlic and chilli flakes into a mixing bowl. Add the olive oil and vinegar, if using, then tear in half of the basil. Toss well to coat and set aside.

4. Pop the focaccia slices under the grill for 3–4 minutes, or until golden and toasted to your liking.

5. In a separate bowl, combine the yoghurt and feta, along with the lemon zest and juice. Add plenty of cracked black pepper and a small pinch of salt to taste. Using the back of a fork, mash the feta into the yoghurt – you want to keep this fairly chunky, so don't mash it too smooth.

6. Once ready to serve, rub the whole garlic clove over the toasted focaccia slices. Spoon the feta yoghurt onto a serving platter, and top with the chickpea and tomato mixture. Garnish with the remaining basil leaves, along with the pine nuts and an extra drizzle of olive oil, if you fancy. Scoop everything up with the grilled focaccia.

> **TOP TIP**
> *Semi-dried tomatoes are softer and juicier than sun-dried tomatoes, with a more intense, sweet-tangy flavour. If you can't find them, just use sun-dried tomatoes.*

CRUNCHY CHICKPEAS, SPICY CAULIFLOWER, WHIPPED FETA + POMEGRANATE SLAW

Feeds 4–6
Takes 50 minutes–1 hour

 SARAH LIVEING

There's so much texture and deliciousness in this dish created by Sarah Liveing, from the crunchy chickpeas to the creamy whipped feta and little juicy bursts of pomegranate in the slaw. As Sarah says, 'Umami isn't just about flavour; foods are also about texture.' This dish hits all the flavour and texture checkpoints.

---

1 medium cauliflower, *left whole, outer leaves removed*
2 tbsp olive oil
1 tsp sea salt
1 heaped tsp ground cumin
1 heaped tsp ground coriander
½ tsp ground turmeric
1 tsp garlic powder
½ tsp smoked paprika
salt and pepper
warm pittas, *to serve*

FOR THE POMEGRANATE SLAW
4 tbsp olive oil
2 tbsp red or white wine vinegar
3 tsp pomegranate molasses / 1 teaspoon honey, *to taste*
2 large carrots, *coarsely grated*
1 small red cabbage, *finely sliced*
100g (3½oz) pomegranate seeds or raisins
10g (¼oz) parsley, *chopped*

FOR THE CHICKPEAS
2 tbsp olive oil
1 tbsp curry powder
570g (1lb 4½oz) jarred chickpeas, *drained and patted dry with a paper towel*

FOR THE WHIPPED FETA
200g (7oz) feta cheese
2 tbsp lemon juice
½ tsp garlic powder / 1 small garlic clove, *grated*

1. Find a deep saucepan big enough to fit the whole cauliflower and half-fill with salted water. Bring to the boil, then add the cauliflower, stalk side up, making sure the cauliflower is fully immersed in the water. Boil for 10 minutes until just tender. Drain and let the cauliflower steam dry for a few minutes. This par-boiling step ensures a meltingly soft inside while allowing the oven to crisp up the outside.

2. Preheat your oven to 200°C/180°C fan/400°F/gas mark 6 and line a shallow roasting tin or large baking tray with baking paper.

3. In a large mixing bowl, combine the olive oil, salt and all the spices. Place the cauliflower in the prepared tin, pour over the spice mixture, then use your hands to rub it all over the cauliflower until fully coated.

4. In the same bowl, add the oil and curry powder for the chickpeas with a pinch of salt and mix to combine. Tip in the chickpeas and stir to coat. Tumble the chickpeas into the tray with the cauliflower, making sure they're scattered evenly. Roast in the oven for 30–35 minutes, or until the cauliflower is golden and the chickpeas are crispy. The chickpeas may pop in the oven – this is totally normal and will make them extra crispy.

5. To make the slaw, whisk together the oil, vinegar and 2 teaspoons of the pomegranate molasses (or 1 teaspoon of honey) in a large bowl. Add the remaining slaw ingredients and toss everything in the dressing. Taste and season, adding more molasses (or honey) if you like it sweeter. Leave this for as long as you can – the longer you leave it, the softer it will be.

6. To make the whipped feta, put all the ingredients into a blender or food processor with 3 tablespoons of water and blitz until you reach a smooth, thick, spreadable consistency. Add another splash or two of water to loosen, if necessary.

7. Make the herb dressing by mixing all the ingredients together in a bowl. Taste for seasoning and adjust as needed.

8. Once the cauliflower and chickpeas are golden and crispy, remove from the oven and let them cool a little before serving.

1 tbsp dried oregano

2 tbsp tahini

FOR THE HERB DRESSING

20g (¾oz) parsley leaves, *chopped*

1 large clove garlic, *finely grated*

½ tsp sea salt

1 tsp za'atar or dried oregano

2 tbsp white wine vinegar

3 tbsp olive oil

9. To serve, spread the whipped feta over a serving dish and place the cauliflower in the centre. Spoon over the herby dressing, then serve the crispy chickpeas, the slaw and some warm pittas alongside.

TOP TIP

You can make the slaw ahead of time to allow the flavours to mellow. Pop it in the refrigerator if you're making it the day before.

SMASHED CHICKPEAS ON TOAST WITH FRIED EGG + PICKLED CUCUMBERS

Feeds 2
Takes 20 minutes

FRED LEEMING

This upgraded toast was dreamed up by Fred Leeming, founder Amelia's husband – who spent six months riding a motorbike through China, hellbent on tasting ALL the local cuisine. It's bursting with flavour and texture, thanks to the creamy chickpeas, spicy fried egg and tangy cucumbers – it's Amelia's all-time favourite brunch dish.

---

1 tbsp neutral oil, such as sunflower or rapeseed oil

1–2 tsp crispy chilli oil

1 tbsp sesame seeds

2 large eggs (or 4 medium if extra hungry)

4 slices sourdough bread, toasted

handful of coriander, roughly chopped

1–2 spring onions, thinly sliced

salt and pepper

FOR THE PICKLED CUCUMBER

100ml (3½fl oz) white wine or apple cider vinegar

100ml (3½fl oz) water

2 tbsp granulated sugar

2 tbsp fine salt

1 cucumber, very thinly sliced

1 large carrot, very thinly sliced or peeled into ribbons

3 garlic cloves, roughly chopped into large chunks

1 tsp dried chilli flakes

FOR THE CHICKPEAS

½ × 570g (1lb 4½oz) jarred chickpeas, drained

2 tbsp cream cheese

2 tsp sesame oil

1. To make the pickled cucumbers, combine the vinegar, water, sugar and salt in a small saucepan and bring to the boil. Combine the cucumber slices, carrot ribbons, garlic chunks and chilli flakes in a large jar, then pour in the vinegar mixture. Leave to pickle, ideally for at least 24 hours, before serving.

2. When you're ready to cook, roughly mash the chickpeas in a bowl, leaving some chunks. Stir in the cream cheese, sesame oil and a little splash of pickling juice from the cucumber jar. Season to taste with salt and lots of black pepper, and mix until creamy yet textured.

3. Heat the neutral oil, crispy chilli oil and sesame seeds in a frying pan over a medium heat. Crack in the eggs and fry for about 3 minutes until the edges are crispy and the yolk is done to your liking. Baste the eggs with some of the cooking oils for extra flavour and crispiness.

4. Divide the smashed chickpeas between the slices of toasted sourdough and spread to cover. Add a layer of pickled cucumbers, then top with the fried eggs and garnish with the coriander and spring onions.

TOP TIP

The pickled cucumbers will keep in the refrigerator for up to 3 months, and taste fab in a sandwich, scattered over a salad or with an omelette.

CHICKPEA, SWEET POTATO + PEANUT BUTTER CURRY

Feeds 3–4
Takes 40 minutes

Our favourite part of this recipe – one of our top-rated ones from the website – is that the sweet potatoes are gently poached in coconut milk and all those sweet and spicy aromatics, so it's full-on flavour from the inside out. The peanut butter adds an extra layer of creaminess, as do the chickpeas. If you're looking for pure comfort, THIS is it!

---

1 tbsp coconut oil or neutral oil, such as sunflower or rapeseed oil

1 onion, roughly chopped

3 garlic cloves, grated

thumb-sized piece of fresh ginger, peeled and grated

1 tsp ground cumin

1 tsp ground turmeric

2 tsp garam masala

1 tsp chilli powder (optional)

½ tsp cinnamon / 1 cinnamon stick

500g (1lb 2oz) sweet potato, butternut squash or pumpkin, peeled and cut into chunks

400ml (14fl oz) can coconut milk

100ml (3½fl oz) veg stock

2 tbsp peanut butter

200g (7oz) fresh spinach

100g (3½oz) sugar snap peas

700g (1lb 9oz) jarred chickpeas, with their bean stock

juice of ½ lime, plus wedges to serve

15g (½oz) coriander, roughly chopped

salt and pepper

TO SERVE (OPTIONAL)

Greek or natural yoghurt

mango chutney

roasted peanuts or toasted flaked almonds, roughly chopped

cooked white or brown rice

warm naans or flat breads

1. Heat the coconut oil in a large saucepan over a medium heat. Add the onion and cook for about 8 minutes until softened, then add the garlic and ginger and cook for 2 minutes more until fragrant.

2. Add the cumin, turmeric, garam masala, chilli powder and cinnamon, along with a splash of water, and stir to create a paste. Cook for 1–2 minutes until fragrant.

3. Add the sweet potato, squash or pumpkin chunks, along with the coconut milk and veg stock. Bring to the boil, then reduce the heat and simmer, uncovered, for 25–30 mins until the liquid has reduced right down and the starch has leached from the sweet potatoes (or squash or pumpkin cubes) to create a thick sauce. They should be soft enough that a cutlery knife can be inserted into the centre easily.

4. Stir in the peanut butter until it mellows into the sauce. If your peanut butter is particularly thick, try mixing it with a splash of water first to loosen it into a runnier paste so it is easier to stir in. Add the spinach, sugar snaps and chickpeas, along with their stock – you may need to add the spinach in batches. Mix well to combine, then simmer for 2–3 minutes, or until the spinach has wilted. Add the lime juice and most of the coriander, saving a handful for a garnish. Check for seasoning, adding salt, pepper and more lime juice, if desired.

5. Serve the curry into bowls, and top with the remaining coriander, along with a dollop of yoghurt, some mango chutney and a scattering of roasted nuts for crunch, if you fancy. Serve with cooked rice and naans or flat breads for something even heartier, if you like.

CHICKPEA, TOMATO + HARISSA STEW WITH HERBY YOGHURT

Feeds 2
Takes 20 minutes

This is an iconic Bold Bean dish. Sweet cherry tomatoes, spicy harissa and chickpeas make an absolute banger of a dish — and it only takes 20 minutes. The tomatoes get blistered and charred so they're bursting with flavour, the bean stock makes everything super saucy and the harissa kick is balanced with creamy, herby yoghurt.

2 tbsp olive oil

250g (9oz) cherry or baby plum tomatoes

2 garlic cloves, *finely sliced*

570g (1lb 4½oz) jarred chickpeas, *with their bean stock*

2 tbsp good-quality harissa paste

FOR THE HERBY YOGHURT

2 garlic cloves, *grated*

zest of 1 lemon and a squeeze of the juice

15g (½oz) dill or parsley, *finely chopped*

3 tsp capers / a handful of green olives, *drained and chopped*

250g (9oz) Greek yoghurt

TO SERVE (OPTIONAL)

warm flatbreads

couscous or quinoa

1. Heat the olive oil in a non-stick frying pan over a high heat. Add the cherry tomatoes and cook for 5–6 minutes until blistered, soft and slightly charred. Lower the heat to medium, then add the garlic and fry for 1–2 minutes, stirring, until fragrant.

2. Add the chickpeas, along with their bean stock, and bubble for 3–4 minutes until reduced by half. Stir through the harissa and simmer for 2–3 minutes more.

3. Meanwhile, in a bowl, mix together all the ingredients for the herby yoghurt. Adjust the seasoning and acidity to your taste, adding a squeeze of lemon juice if you like it very lemony.

4. Spoon the chickpeas into warm bowls and top with the herby yoghurt. Serve with warm flatbreads and/or cooked couscous or quinoa, if you like.

TOP TIP

If you want some extra veg, stir a couple of handfuls of spinach, sliced chard or kale into the chickpeas when you add the harissa.

QUEEN CHICKPEA BLT SALAD

Feeds 2
Takes 35 minutes

This salad takes all the components of a good BLT and turns it into one heck of a salad. Tomatoey sweetness and crunchy garlic bread croutons contrast so well with the salty bacon and tangy soured cream dressing. Try it, and transform an iconic sandwich into an even more epic salad.

400g (14oz) cherry tomatoes

2 tbsp olive oil

dash of sherry or balsamic vinegar

2 slices bread (*we love sourdough or baguette*), *cut into chunky croutons*

2 garlic cloves, *finely grated*

6–8 streaky bacon rashers

570g (1lb 4½oz) jarred chickpeas, *drained*

1 romaine or butter lettuce, *roughly chopped*

salt and pepper

FOR THE DRESSING

75g (2¾oz) soured cream

25g (1oz) Parmesan or vegetarian hard cheese, *finely grated, plus shavings to serve*

10g (¼oz) chives, *finely chopped*

zest and juice of ½ lemon

1. Preheat your oven to 180°C/160°C fan/350°F/gas mark 4.

2. Put the tomatoes in a deep roasting dish. Toss well with 1 tablespoon of the olive oil, a dash of vinegar and a good pinch of salt and pepper.

3. Tumble the bread chunks onto another tray. Add the remaining oil and the garlic, and toss to coat.

4. Put the garlic bread croutons on the top shelf of the oven and the tomatoes underneath. Cook for about 10 minutes, tossing the croutons halfway through, until they are crispy.

5. Meanwhile, line a baking tray with baking parchment and lay the bacon rashers across it.

6. Remove the croutons from the oven and set aside. Add the chickpeas to the roasting dish with the tomatoes and return to the oven. Add the tray of bacon to the oven too, placing it on the top shelf. Cook for 10–15 minutes until the tomatoes are softened and just beginning to burst, and the bacon is crispy.

7. Meanwhile, combine all the ingredients for the dressing in a small bowl and season to taste.

8. When everything is ready, add the lettuce and croutons to a salad bowl, along with the roasted tomatoes and chickpeas. Break the bacon into the bowl in large shards, then pour in most of the dressing and toss everything together so that the lettuce gets nicely coated. Drizzle the remaining dressing on top and finish with extra shavings of Parmesan, if you like, and some cracked black pepper.

ONE-PAN CHICKPEA, ROASTED GRAPE + CARAMELISED CARROT WITH BAKED FETA

Feeds 3–4 as a light meal
Takes 1 hour 5 minutes

Remember the baked feta hype? This one's beanier and better. If you've never thought about caramelising your carrots, do try this, because they go SO well with creamy chickpeas, baked with sweet, juicy grapes. This also works perfectly with parsnips. This is a sweet, warm salad for a cold evening with plenty of leftovers for lunch.

4–5 carrots, *chopped on the diagonal into 2cm (¾in) chunks*

4 tbsp olive oil

1 tsp sumac

300g (10½oz) seedless red grapes

570g (1lb 4½oz) jarred chickpeas, *rinsed, drained and patted dry with a paper towel*

200g (7oz) feta

1 tsp dried oregano

100g (3½oz) kale

50g (1¾oz) pumpkin seeds

15g (½oz) dill or parsley, *roughly chopped*

salt and pepper

FOR THE DRESSING

juice of 1 lemon

½ tsp sumac

½ tsp dried oregano

½ tsp honey

1. Preheat the oven to 200°C/180°C fan/400°F/gas mark 6. Tip the carrots into a large roasting tray and toss with 2 tablespoons of the olive oil and the sumac. Season well. Cover with foil and cook for an initial 25 minutes. Covering with foil helps bring out their natural sweetness, as it cooks them in their own juices.

2. After 25 minutes, remove the foil from the tray and toss in the grapes, chickpeas and a pinch of salt. Give everything a good stir. Nestle the block of feta in the centre of the tray, drizzle with another tablespoon of the oil, then sprinkle the whole tray with the oregano. Roast, uncovered, for a further 25–30 minutes until the carrots are caramelised, the grapes are near to bursting and the feta is golden and caramelised on top.

3. For this dish, we've made it easy by keeping it all in one pan – the kale doesn't get quite as crispy this way, but we sort of like the half-steamed-half-crispy situation. If you prefer crispiness, opt for roasting the kale in a second tray, moving the carrots to the oven shelf below – otherwise, continue here! Once the carrots have softened and the grapes are bursting, remove from the oven, lay the kale on top, drizzle with the remaining oil and season with a pinch of salt and pepper. Top with the pumpkin seeds and return to the oven for a further 5 minutes, or until the kale is crispy and the pumpkin seeds are bursting.

4. Meanwhile, in a small bowl, mix together all the ingredients for the dressing – we're not adding any oil, because we've already got plenty in the traybake.

5. When the traybake is ready, use the back of a fork or spoon to break up the feta a bit. Pour the dressing into the tray and toss to fully coat all the ingredients. Finish with dill or parsley.

TOP TIP

This is a great one to take for lunch as it reheats super well. It's also just as banging eaten cold, stuffed into some pittas to make more of the leftovers.

THE SALAD JAR

Let's face it, lunchtime is the highlight of the working day – especially when you've already prepped something DELICIOUS that you just know is going to hit the spot.

Enter: the salad jar. By using a jar, you can create height, layering up the ingredients so every section stays crisp and delicious. Soggy salad leaves? Not here!

Keep a couple of clean, empty 570g (1lb 4½oz) jars (our Bold Bean ones are perfect) on hand to assemble your salad in. The dressings may thicken in the refrigerator, so we suggest removing the jars at least 15 minutes before serving. Simply tip onto a plate and toss to coat.

BEETROOT + BORLOTTI BEANS

8 finely chopped sun-dried tomatoes

2 tbsp balsamic vinegar

zest and juice of ½ lemon

4 tbsp extra virgin olive oil

570g (1lb 4½oz) jarred borlotti beans, *drained*

250g (9oz) beetroot, *cooked and chopped*

100g (3½oz) goats' cheese

2 handfuls of spinach

a handful of blanched hazelnuts or walnuts, *toasted and roughly chopped*

1. Put the sun-dried tomatoes into a bowl, along with the balsamic vinegar, lemon zest and juice, and the olive oil. Whisk together to create a dressing.

2. Stir the beans through the dressing. Season to taste.

3. It's now time to get layering. Divide the dressed beans between 2 clean, empty jars. Divide the beetroot between each jar, followed by the goats' cheese. Add a handful of spinach to each jar.

4. To finish, top each jar with a handful of the hazelnuts or walnuts. Screw on the lid, and you're good to go.

MISO BLACK BEANS WITH CHICKEN + LIME

1 tbsp white miso

small thumb-sized piece of fresh ginger

pinch of dried chilli flakes

4 tbsp extra virgin olive oil

juice of 1½ limes

570g (1lb 4½oz) jarred black beans, drained

large handful of coriander, chopped

250g (9oz) chicken, cooked and shredded

1 avocado, cut into cubes

100g (3½oz) raw crunchy veg, chopped
(we like sugar snap peas, mangetout and radishes)

handful of salted cashews, roughly chopped

---

1. Put the white miso into a bowl. Finely grate in the ginger, then add a pinch of dried chilli flakes, the olive oil and most of the lime juice. Whisk together to create a dressing.

2. Stir in the black beans and the coriander (stalks and all), and season to taste.

3. Divide the chicken between 2 clean, empty jars. Top with the dressed black beans, followed by the avocado, and squeeze over the remaining lime juice. Layer in the raw crunchy veg.

4. To finish, top with a handful of the salted cashews before screwing on the lids.

THE SALAD JAR

THE SALAD JAR continued

CURRIED CHICKPEAS + AUBERGINE

1 tsp curry powder

3 tbsp mango chutney

4 tbsp lemon juice

2 tsp cumin seeds, *toasted*

4 tbsp extra virgin olive oil

100g (3½oz) cherry tomatoes, *chopped*

3 spring onions, *sliced (both green and white parts)*

½ cucumber, *chopped*

570g (1lb 4½oz) jarred chickpeas, *drained*

⅛ red cabbage, *shredded or coarsely grated*

a slice of chargrilled aubergine from a jar

handful of mint leaves

1. Mix together the curry powder, 1 tablespoon of the mango chutney, the lemon juice, the cumin seeds and olive oil in a bowl.

2. Add the chopped cherry tomatoes, the spring onions, the cucumber and the chickpeas. Stir and season to taste.

3. Divide the dressed chickpeas and veggies between 2 clean, empty jars. Add half of the red cabbage to each jar.

4. To finish, add a slice of chargrilled aubergine to each one, along with another spoonful of mango chutney and a handful of mint leaves. Screw on the lids and you're done.

AJI VERDE GREENS + WHITE BEANS

30g (1oz) coriander

½–1 green chilli, *chopped*

4 tbsp mayonnaise or Greek yoghurt

juice of 1 lime

1 baby gem lettuce, *leaves separated*

570g (1lb 4½oz) jarred white beans, *drained*

200g (7oz) Tenderstem broccoli, *roasted or blanched*

75g (2¾oz) feta, *crumbled*

½ raw courgette, *peeled lengthways into ribbons*

handful of pumpkin seeds, *toasted*

---

1. In a blender, combine the coriander (stalks and all) with the green chilli (depending on how spicy you like it), the mayonnaise or Greek yoghurt and the lime juice. Blitz to create a vivid green dressing, and season to taste.

2. Tear the baby gem lettuce leaves into chunky pieces in a bowl. Pour over the dressing and toss together.

3. Divide the white beans between 2 clean, empty jars. Top with the dressed baby gem, followed by the Tenderstem broccoli, crumbled feta and the courgette ribbons.

4. To finish, top with a handful of toasted pumpkin seeds and screw on the lids.

GUT HEALTH EXPERT

"I CAN'T STRESS IT ENOUGH: FIBRE IS THE KEY NUTRIENT WE ALL NEED TO BE EATING MORE OF, AND BEANS ARE ONE OF THE TOP SOURCES OF FIBRE YOU CAN GET."

– Dr Emily Leeming

BORLOTTI BEANS

We're obsessed with the texture and flavour of these freckled, speckled Italian beauties – a little bit chalky, mild, sweet and nutty.

BORLOTTI BEANS CON LE SARDE

Feeds 2–3 as a light main
Takes 25 minutes

This is a fresh take on the Sicilian *pasta con le sarde,* which carefully balances its *agrodolce* (sweet and sour) flavours. Here, we have sultanas for sweetness and red wine vinegar for sourness – a punchy harmony of flavour. Cooked alongside a store-cupboard staple of good-quality sardines, this is an ideal dinner for a summer evening.

---

3 tbsp olive oil

50g (1¾oz) panko breadcrumbs

1 onion, *finely diced*

1 fennel bulb, *finely sliced*

2 fat garlic cloves, *crushed*

½ tsp dried chilli flakes (optional)

40g (1½oz) raisins or sultanas

2–3 tbsp good-quality red wine or sherry vinegar

570g (1lb 4½oz) jarred borlotti beans or chickpeas, *drained*

2 × 120g (4¼oz) cans good-quality sardines in olive oil

15g (½oz) parsley, *roughly chopped*

40g (1½oz) pine nuts, *toasted*

salt and pepper

rocket salad, dressed in lemon and olive oil, *to serve (optional)*

1. Heat 1 tablespoon of the olive oil in a small frying pan over a medium heat. Tip in the panko breadcrumbs and toast, stirring frequently, for 3–4 minutes until golden and crispy. Set aside.

2. Heat the remaining olive oil in a large frying pan over a medium heat. Add the onion, along with a pinch of salt, and stir to coat in the oil. Cook for 3 minutes, then add the fennel and cook for another 10–12 minutes, stirring every now and then, until softened and caramelised. Add the garlic and cook for a further 2 minutes until fragrant. (This part can even be done in the morning to make the speediest dinner when you get in from work!)

3. Add the chilli flakes, if using, along with the raisins or sultanas and vinegar. Mix well to combine and cook for 2 minutes more, stirring often. Pour in the drained borlotti beans and stir to fully coat with the other ingredients.

4. Add the sardines and gently break them up into slightly smaller chunks – not too small or they'll disintegrate, and you want to keep some pieces fairly chunky for texture. Lastly, add the parsley and the pine nuts, along with some cracked black pepper. Mix well to combine and let it all cook for a final 2–3 minutes to let the flavours meld together.

5. Spoon into serving dishes and sprinkle over the crispy breadcrumbs. Serve alongside rocket leaves, simply dressed in lemon and olive oil.

TOP TIP

If your sardines come in lovely olive oil, use this in the recipe instead of regular olive oil. Chickpeas also work wonderfully well in this dish if you don't have any borlotti beans.

BORLOTTI ALLA NORMA WITH CREAMY RICOTTA

Feeds 3
Takes 45 minutes

Borlotti beans are the ideal flavour partners for this aubergine-laden pasta sauce traditionally from the Italian island of Sicily. The aubergines absorb all the tasty goodness you coat them in and, when finished with a flurry of pecorino or Parmesan, this will make you feel like you've been plonked right into the heart of Sicily.

2 aubergines, *chopped into rough 4cm (1½in) chunks*

5 tbsp extra virgin olive oil, *plus extra for drizzling*

1 red or brown onion, *thinly sliced*

4 garlic cloves, *finely sliced*

400g (14oz) can good-quality chopped tomatoes

1 tsp sherry vinegar or red wine vinegar

1 tsp caster sugar *(optional)*

1 tsp dried oregano

½ tsp dried chilli flakes, *adjust to taste*

1 tbsp baby capers

handful of pitted olives *(optional)*

15g (½oz) basil, *leaves picked*

570g (1lb 4½oz) jarred borlotti beans, *with their bean stock*

50g (1¾oz) pecorino or Parmesan or vegetarian hard cheese

250g (9oz) ricotta or buffalo mozzarella, *to serve*

salt and pepper

1. Preheat the oven to 180°C/160°C fan/350°F/gas mark 4. Tumble the aubergine chunks into a large roasting dish and coat generously with 3 tablespoons of the olive oil (this is key to achieving the aubergine's soft melting texture) and a good pinch of salt. Toss well using your hands, then roast for 30–35 minutes until softened.

2. Meanwhile, heat the remaining olive oil in a large frying pan over a medium heat. Once hot, add the onion, along with a pinch of salt, and stir to coat in the oil. Cook for 8–10 minutes until softened and starting to caramelise, stirring occasionally. Add the garlic and cook for a further 2 minutes until fragrant and soft.

3. Add the tomatoes, then fill the can about a third full of water, give it a swirl, and throw that in too, along with the vinegar and another pinch of salt. If your tomatoes aren't top quality, add the sugar for balance. Increase the heat to medium–high to get things bubbling. Stir well, then add the oregano, chilli flakes, capers, olives, if using, and most of the basil leaves (saving a few for a garnish). Let it bubble for 10–12 minutes, stirring occasionally, until the sauce reduces to a glossy consistency. Don't worry if it looks a bit thick – you'll be adding the bean stock soon.

4. Check the aubergine – it should be nice and soft by now. Add it to the frying pan, along with the borlotti beans and their stock, and stir to combine. Simmer for 2–3 minutes to warm the beans. (If you want to freeze the base, now is the time. Be sure to let it cool before you transfer to the freezer.) Finally, add half the pecorino or Parmesan. Stir until melted, then season well with salt and cracked black pepper.

5. Divide between bowls, then sprinkle over the remaining pecorino or Parmesan, and serve with the ricotta or mozzarella. Finish with the remaining basil leaves and another drizzle of olive oil.

TOP TIP

This is a great meal to eat with friends – double the quantities, and roast the aubergine and make the sauce in advance. Reheat with the beans when you are ready to eat.

CACIO E PEPE BORLOTTI BEANS

Feeds 2
Takes 15 minutes

Romans have been worshipping at the altar of cheese and pepper (aka *cacio e pepe*) for centuries. This simple, creamy, indulgent, delicious combo is a pillar of the four great Roman pastas. We haven't messed around with it, simply swapping out pasta for Italian borlotti beans. Ready in just 15 minutes, this is comfort food at its best.

---

2 tsp black peppercorns
1 tbsp olive oil
2 rosemary sprigs
20g (¾oz) butter
570g (1lb 4½oz) jarred borlotti beans, *with their bean stock*
30g (1oz) Parmesan or vegetarian hard cheese, *finely grated*
zest and juice of ½ lemon

TO SERVE (OPTIONAL)
fresh bitter leaf salad
crusty bread

1. Toast the peppercorns in a dry frying pan over a medium heat for 1–2 minutes until they smell amazing. Tip into a pestle and mortar and leave to cool slightly, then grind until fine.

2. Return the pan to a medium heat and add the olive oil. Add the rosemary sprigs and allow to sizzle in the oil, flipping regularly for 30–40 seconds until crispy and fragrant, but not browned. Remove from the pan and drain on a paper towel.

3. Now add the butter to the pan. Once melted, add the beans and their stock, along with the toasted black pepper. Bubble away for a couple of minutes, stirring all the while, to allow everything to emulsify.

4. Take the pan off the heat and stir through the cheese and a squeeze of lemon juice.

5. Check the seasoning, then serve in bowls. Strip the crispy rosemary leaves and scatter them over the beans, along with the lemon zest. We like to eat this with a fresh bitter leaf salad and some crusty bread.

TOP TIP
If you can't find borlotti beans, butter beans will work just as well, thanks to their creamy indulgence.

SAUSAGE MEATBALLS WITH BORLOTTI BEANS, FENNEL + MOZZARELLA

Feeds 4
Takes 40 minutes

This hug-in-a-bowl one-pan wonder combines creamy borlotti beans with the subtle sweetness of fennel to create a cosy and flavour-packed dish, served with creamy polenta to soak up the delicious sauce. You can also use butter beans for this one – their rich, buttery texture pairs perfectly with these hearty flavours.

---

1 tbsp olive oil, plus extra if needed

1 brown or red onion, thinly sliced

1 fennel bulb, thinly sliced

2 garlic cloves, crushed

1 tbsp tomato purée

400g (14oz) can chopped or cherry tomatoes

1 tsp dried oregano or mixed herbs

570g (1lb 4½oz) jarred borlotti beans, with their bean stock

1 tsp red wine vinegar or balsamic vinegar (optional)

pinch of caster sugar (optional)

150g (5½oz) fresh mozzarella, drained and torn into pieces (optional)

salt and pepper

green salad, to serve

FOR THE MEATBALLS

400g (14oz) sausage meat / good-quality sausages (we love Italian-style or herby ones), skins removed

1 garlic clove, finely grated

1 tsp fennel seeds, lightly crushed

½–1 tsp dried chilli flakes, adjust to taste

2 tbsp finely chopped parsley or chives, plus extra for garnish

1. Preheat the oven to 200°C/180°C fan/400°F/gas mark 6.

2. Begin by making the meatballs. In a large bowl, mix together all the meatball ingredients, stirring until well combined. Using your hands, form the mixture into small meatballs, each about the size of a golf ball.

3. Heat the olive oil in a large ovenproof saucepan over a medium heat. Add the meatballs (in batches so you don't overcrowd the pan) and cook for 8–10 minutes, turning occasionally until golden brown on all sides – they don't need to be fully cooked yet. Don't stress if they fall apart a little, but if they are really sticking, add a splash more oil. Once cooked, use tongs to remove the meatballs to a plate, leaving all their juices and nuggets of flavour in the pan.

4. Add a little more olive oil to the pan if needed, then add the onion and fennel, along with a pinch of salt, and cook for 10–15 minutes, stirring occasionally, until soft and beginning to caramelise at the bottom of the pan. Add the garlic and cook for another 2 minutes until fragrant.

5. Stir in the tomato purée and cook for 1–2 minutes, then add the chopped tomatoes and dried oregano. Season and stir to combine. Simmer for 5–7 minutes, allowing the flavours to meld and the sauce to thicken slightly.

6. Now add the borlotti beans, along with their bean stock, and bring to a simmer. At this point, taste the sauce; if it needs a bit more acidity, add the vinegar, or if it needs a bit more sweetness, add a pinch of sugar.

7. Nestle the browned meatballs back into the pan among the beans. Tear the fresh mozzarella over the top of the dish, transfer the pan to the oven and bake for 10–12 minutes, or until the meatballs are cooked through and the mozzarella is melted and golden.

8. Meanwhile, make the creamy polenta. Bring the milk to a gentle boil in a saucepan. Gradually whisk in the polenta, still on a medium heat, until the mixture is as thick as mashed potatoes. If it looks too thick, loosen with a splash more milk. Once it's creamy, remove from the heat and stir in the remaining ingredients. Sprinkle with the chives just before serving.

FOR THE CREAMY POLENTA

600ml (20fl oz) milk, *plus a little more if needed*

100g (3½oz) instant polenta

100g (3½oz) salted butter

50g (1¾oz) Parmesan or vegetarian hard cheese, *finely grated*

pinch of cayenne pepper

zest of 1 lemon *(optional)*

2 tbsp chopped chives, *to serve*

9. Scatter the parsley or dill over the meatballs and serve with the creamy polenta and a fresh green salad. A glass of wine wouldn't go amiss either!

TOP TIP
Veggie sausages would work well here, and the dish is still delicious without mozzarella on top, if you want to make a vegetarian version.

BORLOTTI BEANS

SAUSAGE, BROCCOLI + PECORINO BEANS

Feeds 2–3
Takes 30 minutes

Fennel seeds, sausages and beans are a match made in heaven, and this dish makes use of the delicious bean stock to create a saucier texture, while the crispy breadcrumbs add a satisfying crunch. It's ready in 30 minutes and only uses one pot, which means less washing-up and more time on the sofa. Perfect for a moody, misty evening.

---

2 tbsp olive oil

6 good-quality sausages, *skins removed*

2 garlic cloves, *crushed*

1½–2 tsps fennel seeds, *adjust to taste*

100ml (3½fl oz) water

½–1 tsp dried chilli flakes, *adjust to taste*

570g (1lb 4½oz) jarred borlotti beans, *with their bean stock*

1 large head of broccoli, *chopped into florets*

50g (1¾oz) pecorino or Parmesan or vegetarian hard cheese

1 tbsp melted butter or extra virgin olive oil

salt and pepper

FOR THE PANGRATTATO

1 tbsp olive oil

40g (1½oz) fresh breadcrumbs

zest of 1 lemon, *plus wedges to serve*

15g (½oz) parsley, *very finely chopped*

1. Heat the olive oil in a large frying pan, for which you have a lid, over a medium–high heat. Add the sausage meat to the pan and break up into small pieces. Cook for 8–10 minutes until browned and crispy in places.

2. Reduce the heat to medium and add the garlic and fennel seeds. Cook for 1 minute more, then pour in the measured water, along with a pinch of salt and the chilli flakes. Stir to scrape the bottom of the pan and release the flavourful brown bits, then add the beans with their bean stock. Bring to a simmer, then tumble the broccoli on top and cover the pan with a lid to let the broccoli steam for about 6 minutes until it is bright green but still has some bite to it.

3. While your broccoli is cooking, make your pangrattato. Heat the olive oil in a small frying pan over a medium heat. Add the breadcrumbs and cook for 3 minutes, stirring often, until golden, making sure they don't burn. Stir in the lemon zest and parsley and season to taste.

4. When the broccoli is ready, turn off the heat. Remove the lid from the pan and scatter over the pecorino or Parmesan, season with black pepper and drizzle over the melted butter or extra virgin olive oil.

5. Divide into bowls and top with a sprinkling of the pangrattato, then serve with lemon wedges for squeezing over.

> **TOP TIP**
> *Making breadcrumbs is a great way to use up stale bread or the ends of bread – simply blitz in a food processor. If your bread is too soft, you can toast it before blitzing.*

SPICED ONION + BORLOTTI BEAN FRITTATA

Feeds 4
Takes 25 minutes

MARK WHENMAN

Onions and eggs are a classic combination. Here, Mark Whenman is ramping it up a gear by adding chilli paste – opt for chipotle if you want a smoky flavour – and, of course, lots of beans. He says, 'This borlotti bean frittata is a perfect example of how simple ingredients can come together to create something unexpectedly delicious.'

---

1 tbsp olive oil
2 small onions, *finely chopped*
2 garlic cloves, *finely chopped*
1 tbsp harissa or chipotle paste, *adjust to taste*
1 tsp smoked paprika
1 tsp ground cumin
570g (1lb 4½oz) jarred borlotti beans, *drained and rinsed*
6 large eggs
75g (2¾oz) Cheddar or Gruyère cheese, *grated*
salt and pepper

TO SERVE
handful of parsley or coriander leaves, *finely chopped*
fresh salad leaves, *dressed in olive oil and lemon juice or balsamic vinegar*
crusty bread *(optional)*

1. Heat the olive oil in a large, high-sided, ovenproof frying pan over a medium–low heat. Add the onions and cook for 8–10 minutes, stirring occasionally, until softened.

2. Add the garlic, harissa or chipotle paste and spices, and cook for a further 5 minutes until fragrant.

3. Lightly pat dry the beans using a clean tea towel, then add them to the pan. (This drying step helps the frittata hold together better. Don't worry if you crush a few beans in the process; that will help bind the mixture more too.) Increase the heat to medium and cook for a few minutes, stirring, until well combined. Then reduce the heat to medium–low and spread everything evenly across the pan.

4. Whisk the eggs in a jug with a good pinch of salt and pepper, then pour into the pan, making sure everything is covered. Give it all a quick stir, then leave to cook, undisturbed, for 5 minutes until the eggs are nearly set and the frittata is turning golden brown on the bottom. While it's cooking, preheat the grill to high.

5. Sprinkle the cheese over the top, then pop under the grill for 1–2 minutes until the cheese bubbles and turns golden.

6. Remove from the grill and allow to cool a little, then use a soft spatula to loosen the edges of the frittata. Carefully slide it out onto a large serving plate. Sprinkle over some chopped fresh parsley or coriander and enjoy with a dressed salad and maybe some crusty bread too.

> **TOP TIP**
> *This recipe is great for making in advance and is easily transportable for a take-to-work lunch. Sub in black beans, if you like – they also work well.*

BORLOTTI BEAN FAJITAS WITH ZESTY AVOCADO CREAM

Feeds 3
Takes 35 minutes

JASVINDER KAUR

Bold Bean bud Jasvinder Kaur remembers the leftover peppers from her dad's weekly food shop: 'I started experimenting with different spice blends, veggies, grains and beans, inspired by my Indian heritage, in a bid to use up the peppers. This recipe is now a long-standing family favourite.' We can assure you, it's a guaranteed crowd-pleaser.

2 tbsp olive oil
1 large red onion, chopped
2 red peppers, cored, deseeded and sliced into strips
150g (5½oz) mushrooms, sliced
1 tbsp tomato purée
2 fat garlic cloves, finely chopped
2 tsp ground cumin
2 tsp paprika
1 tsp cayenne pepper
½ tsp ground cinnamon
½ tsp ground coriander
570g (1lb 4½oz) jarred borlotti beans, drained, bean stock reserved
salt and pepper

FOR THE SALSA
250g (9oz) cherry tomatoes, diced
juice of ½ lime
1 red chilli, deseeded and finely diced
handful of coriander leaves, finely chopped

FOR THE AVOCADO CREAM
1 large ripe avocado, peeled and stoned
2 tbsp Greek or natural yoghurt
juice of ½ lime, plus wedges to serve

TO SERVE
8 soft tortilla wraps
grated Cheddar (optional)
pickled red onions (optional)

1. Heat the olive oil in a large frying pan over a medium heat. Add the red onion, peppers and mushrooms, along with a pinch of salt, and cook for 4–5 minutes until starting to soften. Next, add the tomato purée, garlic and spices, and mix well to coat the veg. Continue to cook for a further 8–10 minutes until the veg is nicely softened and looking a little jammy, stirring occasionally.

2. Meanwhile, prepare the salsa. Combine all the ingredients in a bowl, reserving a little of the coriander for a garnish. Add a good pinch of salt and mix well. Check for seasoning, then set aside.

3. For the avocado cream, combine all the ingredients in a blender with a pinch of salt and blitz until smooth, creamy and slightly whipped. Taste and adjust for seasoning. If you don't have a blender, you can just mash the ripe avocado with a fork, then stir into the yoghurt with the lime juice and salt. It may be a little chunkier, but it works just as well!

4. Once the veg has softened, add the drained borlotti beans. Stir to combine and cook for 3–4 minutes until they are warmed through. If it's looking a little dry, add a splash of the reserved bean stock to loosen.

5. Once you're ready to serve, heat a separate dry frying pan over a medium–high heat and heat the tortilla wraps for a few minutes on each side until warm and a little charred.

6. To serve, spread avocado cream over a warmed wrap, then top with a couple of heaped tablespoons of the borlotti bean mixture and a spoonful of the salsa, followed by some coriander and a squeeze of lime. Finish with any additional toppings you fancy – we like grated Cheddar and pickled red onions – then fold up and enjoy.

FRESH PESTO BORLOTTIS WITH CHARGRILLED COURGETTES + TOMATOES

Feeds 4–6
Takes 1 hour 15 minutes

Our borlotti salad is a feast of a summer salad in its own right – packed with charred summer veggies and buttery borlotti beans dressed in a vibrant pesto – but it's also ideal as a barbecue centrepiece, served with marinated chicken thighs or halloumi. If you don't have borlotti beans, opt for butter beans, which have a similar creamy texture.

FOR THE MARINATED CHICKEN/HALLOUMI

zest and juice of 1 lemon, and slices of 1 more
3 garlic cloves, *finely chopped*
1½ tsp honey
1 tsp dried chilli flakes
1 tbsp dried oregano
2 tbsp extra virgin olive oil
8–10 skinless and boneless chicken thighs / 200g (7oz) halloumi, *drained*
salt and pepper

FOR THE SALAD

750g (1lb 10oz) cherry tomatoes, *halved*
4 tbsp olive oil
4 courgettes, *thinly sliced lengthways into long ribbons using a veg peeler or mandolin*
2 × 570g (1lb 4½oz) jarred borlotti beans (or butter beans), *drained*
120g (4¼oz) rocket leaves

FOR THE PESTO

50g (1¾oz) pine nuts or pumpkin seeds
80g (2¾oz) basil
50g (1¾oz) Parmesan or vegetarian hard cheese
150ml (5fl oz/¼ pint) olive oil
2 garlic cloves

TO SERVE (OPTIONAL)
tzatziki or Greek yoghurt

1. First, make the marinade. Put the lemon zest and juice, garlic, honey, chilli flakes, oregano and olive oil in a large bowl and mix to combine. Season the chicken or halloumi and cut into large cubes. Pour the marinade over, rubbing it in to coat each piece well. Leave to marinate for at least 15 minutes (or overnight in the refrigerator for deeper flavour).

2. Preheat the oven to 190°C/170°C fan/375°F/gas mark 5.

3. For the salad, arrange the cherry tomatoes on a baking tray, cut-sides up. Drizzle with 2 tablespoons of the olive oil and season. Roast for 45 minutes, or until caramelised and slightly crinkled.

4. Meanwhile, toss the courgette ribbons in a separate bowl with the remaining olive oil and a pinch of salt and pepper. Set aside.

5. Now make the pesto. Toast the pine nuts in a dry frying pan over a medium heat for about 2 minutes, until lightly golden. Add them to a blender, along with the remaining pesto ingredients, and blitz until smooth. Season to taste and set aside in a large mixing bowl.

6. Preheat the barbecue, or heat a griddle pan over a medium heat. Thread the chicken or halloumi onto skewers, alternating with slices of lemon – the lemon will char on the grill, adding a smoky, citrussy depth that is unbeatable! Put the skewers directly onto the grill or griddle pan and cook for about 12 minutes (8–10 minutes for the halloumi), turning frequently until the meat is cooked through and the juices run clear. When golden and sizzling, remove from the grill.

7. Arrange the courgette ribbons on the grill or in the griddle pan in a single layer – you may need to do this in batches. Grill for 2–3 minutes on either side until they have even char marks.

8. Once the courgette ribbons are ready, pour the drained beans into the bowl with the pesto and mix well to coat. Arrange the pesto beans in layers on a large serving platter with the rocket, roasted tomatoes and grilled courgettes. Serve with tzatziki or Greek yoghurt, if you like, and the chicken or halloumi, along with any other favourite barbecue sides.

SPEEDY TUNA + BORLOTTI BEAN SALAD

Feeds 2
Takes 15 minutes

This recipe takes inspiration from Niçoise-style salads, but swaps the egg for beans — they are packed with protein and bring a hit of creaminess without the need to reach for the mayo. Plus you get a satisfying little hit of salt with every bite of caper and green olive. Oh, and it only takes a few minutes to prepare, so it's both quick and delicious!

½ **red onion,** very thinly sliced

zest of 1 lemon, juice of 2

570g (1lb 4½oz) **jarred borlotti beans,** drained and rinsed

30g (1oz) **parsley,** finely chopped

10g (¼oz) **basil leaves,** torn

1 tbsp **capers or caper berries,** drained

60g (2¼oz) **pitted olives, halved** (Halkidiki or Kalamata olives are our favourites)

200g (7oz) **can good-quality tuna in olive oil,** drained

2 tbsp **extra virgin olive oil**

salt and pepper

1. Put the sliced onion in a bowl with the juice of 1 lemon, and leave to sit for about 10 minutes while you prep the other ingredients — this will reduce the sharpness.

2. Combine all the remaining ingredients except the tuna and oil in a large mixing bowl and toss well to combine. Add the onions too, leaving the lemon juice in the bowl to be discarded.

3. Fold in the tuna, trying to keep it fairly chunky. Now add the olive oil (you could add a little of the oil from the tuna can if it's particularly good quality), along with a generous amount of cracked black pepper, and toss everything well to coat. Taste for seasoning, adding the extra lemon juice if it needs it, then serve.

TOP TIP

This is a fantastic take-to-work lunch. To bulk it out a little, some spinach leaves would be a delicious addition, and a few semi-dried tomatoes would bring a touch of sweetness.

FIVE-STEP MEALS

We all love a simple supper that still packs a punch.

With this easy-to-follow formula, you can pick and choose ingredients already in your refrigerator and cupboards to create epic flavour combos. Ultimately, this formula is designed for you to go your own way but, if you don't know where to begin, try one of our two favourite five-step combos below.

OUR FAVOURITES

CURRIED CAULIFLOWER + BUTTER BEAN FLATBREADS

1. BUTTER BEANS
2. YOUR FAVE CURRY PASTE
3. CAULIFLOWER
4. FLATBREADS
5. CREAMY YOGHURT

CAJUN-SPICED CHICKPEAS AND RICE

1. CHICKPEAS
2. CAJUN SPICE MIX
3. ROOT VEG
4. RICE
5. FRESH HERBS

1. THE BEANS

Choose your fave legume.

- WHITE BEANS
- BUTTER BEANS
- BLACK BEANS
- CHICKPEAS
- CARLIN PEAS

2. FLAVOUR BOMB

Stir through your spices or paste.

- CAJUN SPICE MIX
- MISO PASTE
- BOURSIN
- HARISSA
- CURRY PASTE

3. GREENS/VEG

Roast, steam, pan-fry or serve raw.

- **LEAFY GREENS** — Spinach, rocket, kale
- **GREENS** — Green beans, peas, sugar snap peas
- CAULIFLOWER
- **ROOT VEG** — Carrots, sweet potato, butternut squash
- MEDITERRANEAN VEG

4. PROTEIN/GRAINS

Skip these if you want to keep it light!

- RICE
- FLATBREADS
- COOKED CHICKEN
- CRUSTY BREAD
- BOILED EGG
- CRISPY TOFU

5. FINISHING TOUCHES

Stir through, squeeze or sprinkle.

- FRESHLY SQUEEZED LEMON
- CRUMBLED FETA
- **FRESH HERBS** — Coriander, parsley, dill
- CREAMY YOGHURT
- **TOASTED NUTS** — Cashews, walnuts, almonds

SUSTAINABLE FOOD CHAMPION

"THERE IS NO SILVER BULLET THAT WILL FIX THE FOOD SYSTEM. IT IS COMPLEX AND DEEPLY INTER-CONNECTED. BUT I SOMETIMES THINK A PILL THAT MADE EVERYONE LOVE BEANS WOULD GET PRETTY CLOSE."

– Henry Dimbleby

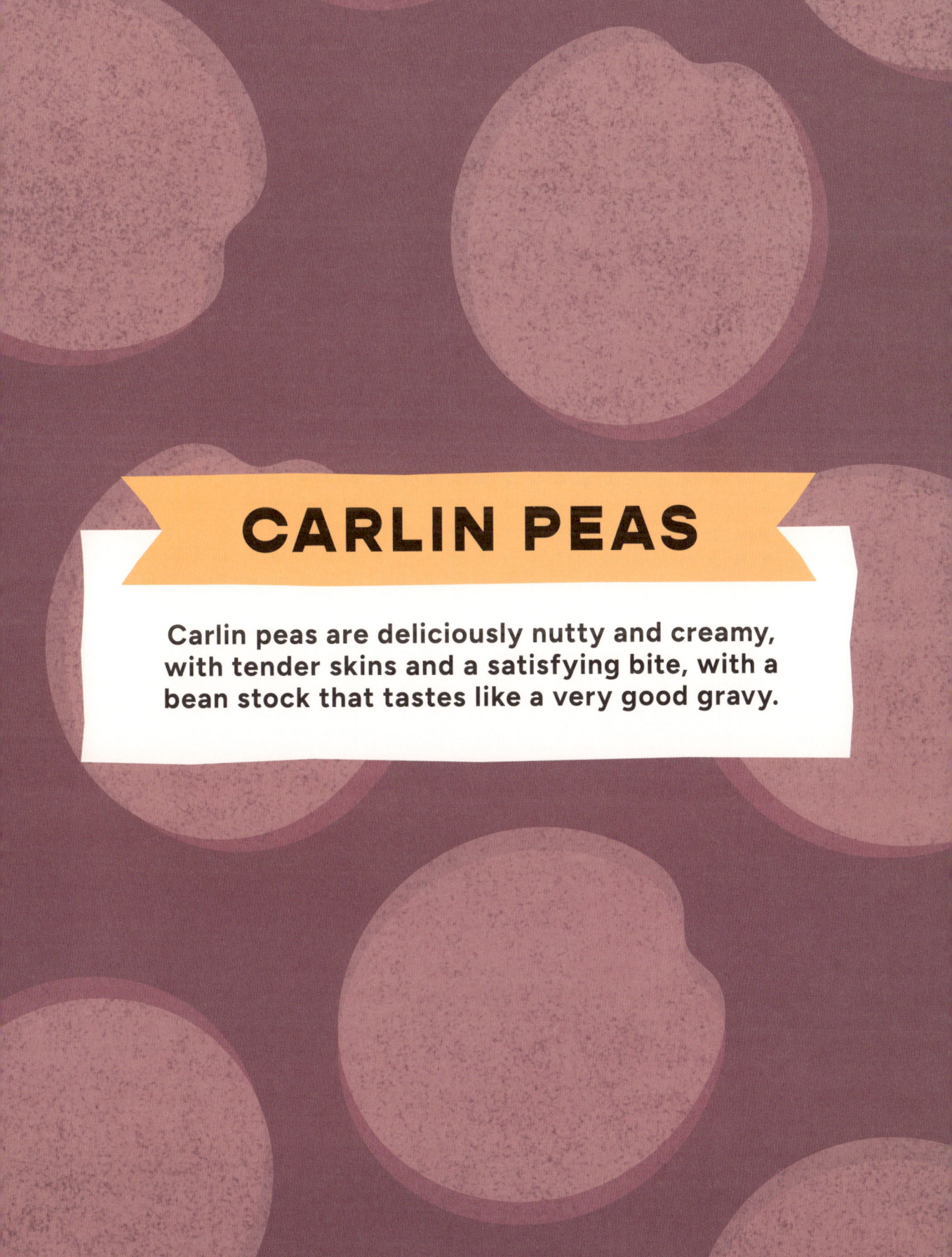

CARLIN PEAS

Carlin peas are deliciously nutty and creamy, with tender skins and a satisfying bite, with a bean stock that tastes like a very good gravy.

DOUBLE PEA TOASTS WITH PEA SMASH, FETA + CRISPY CARLIN PEAS

Feeds 4
Takes 30 minutes

Have you ever roasted carlin peas? Thanks to their smaller surface area, they turn into *the* crispiest nuggets out of all the bean types. They're great on salads, make a fab crunchy snack, and are next-level here, paired with a fresh pea smash on toast with tangy feta, because two types of peas are better than one.

300g (10½oz) frozen peas

½ × 700g (1lb 9oz) jar carlin peas, drained, rinsed and patted dry with a paper towel

2–3 tbsp olive oil, plus extra if needed

1 tsp smoked paprika

1 small garlic clove, peeled

8 mint sprigs, leaves picked

10g (¼oz) fresh chives / 1 spring onion (both green and white parts), roughly chopped

zest of ½ lemon, juice of 1

4 slices of sourdough bread

100g (3½oz) feta

pinch of dried chilli flakes (optional)

salt and pepper

1. Defrost the frozen peas and either microwave for 2 minutes in a heat-proof bowl, or blanch in a saucepan of boiling water for 1–2 minutes. Drain and set aside.

2. The carlin peas can either be roasted or pan-fried – roasting will give you a crisper, crunchier finish, but pan-frying will save on time!

3. If roasting the carlin peas, preheat the oven to 200°C/180°C fan/400°F/gas mark 6. Tip the carlin peas onto a baking tray and toss well with 2 tablespoons of the olive oil and the smoked paprika. Season and roast for 22–25 minutes until super crispy, shaking halfway through.

4. If pan-frying the carlin peas, heat 1 tablespoon of the oil in a frying pan over a medium–high heat. Add the carlin peas and paprika, and fry for about 10 minutes, shaking the pan occasionally, until crispy all over.

5. Meanwhile, make the pea smash. In a food process or blender, combine the cooked peas with the garlic, mint leaves and chives or spring onions. Add the remaining olive oil, along with the lemon zest and juice, and pulse until you have a thick purée (it's good if it's a little chunky). You could also do this in a pestle and mortar for an even chunkier texture. Season to taste and add more olive oil to loosen, if necessary.

6. Toast your bread and spread the purée on top. Scatter over the crispy carlin peas and crumble over the feta. Finish with a pinch of chilli flakes, if you like.

> **TOP TIP**
> *Both the roasted peas and pea smash can be prepared a few hours in advance, making this a speedy assembly job meal.*

FISH FINGER + CURRIED CARLIN PEA SANDOS

Feeds 4
Takes 30 minutes

Carlin peas have a similar taste to an old-school mushy pea, so obviously fish-finger sandos, with curried spices and flaky white fish, are on the cards. Our secret ingredient for the peas is coconut, which adds a fragrant creaminess that makes this nostalgic dish a little more gourmet. If you can't find carlin peas, try marrowfat peas instead.

---

12 good-quality fish fingers

2 tbsp curry paste (mild or spicy)

½ × 570g (1lb 4½oz) jar carlin peas, drained

100ml (3½fl oz) coconut milk or coconut cream

8 thick slices of white bread

1 baby gem lettuce, leaves separated and roughly shredded

salt and pepper

crispy onions, to serve (optional)

FOR THE MAYO

4 tbsp mayonnaise

4 gherkins, thinly sliced

handful of fresh coriander, roughly chopped

juice of 1 lime

1. Preheat the oven and cook the fish fingers according to the packet instructions.

2. While the fish fingers are cooking, heat the curry paste in a saucepan over a low–medium heat. Cook for 1–2 minutes, stirring, until fragrant, then pour in the drained carlin peas and coconut milk or cream. If you're using coconut milk, simmer for 6–7 minutes, allowing the sauce to thicken and coat the peas. If you're using coconut cream, the consistency will be thicker and therefore it will need less simmering time to properly coat the peas, about 4–5 minutes. Season to taste. Remove from the heat and set aside, then roughly mash.

3. Meanwhile, in a small bowl, mix together the mayonnaise, gherkins, coriander and lime juice.

4. To assemble, spread a generous layer of the flavoured mayo on a slice of bread. Top with some shredded lettuce and a layer of the curried carlin peas, then arrange 3 fish fingers on top. Add an extra dollop of mayo or some more lettuce, if you like, and the crispy onions, if using, then sandwich together with another slice of bread. Repeat to make the other sandwiches. Enjoy immediately, while hot and crispy.

> **TOP TIP**
> Double the quantity of carlin peas, adding more coconut milk, some spinach and peas, and serve with rice or naan for an easy one-pot meal.

CARLIN PEA CHAAT

Feeds 4 as a starter
Takes 15 minutes

 RHIA PATEL

If you've never had chaat, you're in for a treat. As Bold Bean Rhia Patel explains, 'Chaat is a classic genre of vegetarian Indian street food that is as much about texture as it is flavour.' Her version uses carlin peas, spiced with cumin, coriander and chilli, as the main event, and brings in tangy sweetness and bright spice with two types of chutney.

570g (1lb 4½oz) jarred carlin peas (or black beans), *drained and rinsed*

2 tsp ground coriander

2 tsp ground cumin

2 tbsp lemon juice

½ tsp chilli powder

salt

FOR THE TAMARIND CHUTNEY

2 tbsp date syrup or honey

2 tbsp tamarind paste

½ tsp chilli powder

FOR THE GREEN CHUTNEY

25g (1oz) mint leaves

25g (1oz) coriander leaves, *plus a handful to garnish*

1 red chilli, *halved and deseeded*

thumb-sized piece of fresh ginger, *grated*

1 small apple, *peeled, cored and roughly chopped*

3 tbsp olive oil

2 tbsp lemon juice

¼ tsp salt

TO SERVE

80g (2¾oz) natural yoghurt

1 small red onion, *finely diced*

2 big handfuls of Bombay mix

30g (1oz) pomegranate seeds

1. To make the tamarind chutney, combine the ingredients in a small bowl and set aside.

2. For the green chutney, combine all the ingredients in a blender and blend until smooth. Taste for seasoning, then set aside. This will make more chutney than you need, but pop into an airtight container in your refrigerator (it will keep for up to 3 days) to add some zing to a cheese toastie, or any other curries on your weekly rota.

3. Add the carlin peas to a saucepan, along with the ground coriander, cumin, chilli powder and lemon juice. Mix well and gently warm through over a low heat for a couple of minutes. Gently mash some of the carlin peas with a fork for a varied texture, then taste and add a little pinch of salt if needed. Tip the contents of the bowl onto a serving plate.

4. To serve, drizzle the yoghurt, tamarind chutney and green chutney onto the peas. Sprinkle over the chopped onion, Bombay mix, pomegranate seeds and remaining coriander leaves to finish.

TOP TIP

If you can't find carlin peas, we suggest using black beans instead – their small, nutty bite works perfectly with the vibrant chutneys and herbs.

CARLIN PEA SAAG WITH MANGO CHUTNEY-GLAZED HALLOUMI

Feeds 3
Takes 30 minutes

Carlin peas perfectly complement this cosy take on saag, a classic dish from Punjab, where greens are simmered with spices to create warm, fragrant flavours. Our version is a blend of saag paneer and dhal, but instead of paneer, we're using halloumi, coated in sweet, sticky, spicy mango chutney. It's creamy and beany!

2 tbsp coconut oil or neutral oil, such as sunflower or rapeseed oil, plus extra if needed

1 tbsp cumin seeds

1 tbsp fennel seeds

1 onion, finely sliced

2 garlic cloves, grated

1 tbsp ground turmeric

1 tbsp mild curry powder

thumb-sized piece of fresh ginger, grated

1 tbsp tomato purée

15g (½oz) coriander, leaves picked and stalks finely chopped

570g (1lb 4½oz) jarred carlin peas, with their bean stock

400ml (14fl oz) can coconut milk

½ veg stock cube (optional)

200g (7oz) spinach

250g (9oz) halloumi, cut into cubes

1 heaped tbsp mango chutney

salt and pepper

TO SERVE

kefir or natural yoghurt, for drizzling (optional)

nigella seeds, for sprinkling (optional)

cooked rice

1. Heat the coconut oil in a large, heavy-based frying pan or skillet over a medium heat. Add the cumin and fennel seeds, and cook for 2 minutes until fragrant and sizzling. Then add the onion, along with a pinch of salt, and cook for 7–8 minutes until softened. If the onion starts to stick, add a splash of water.

2. Add the garlic and cook for a further minute until fragrant, then add the turmeric, curry powder, ginger, tomato purée and coriander stalks, along with a splash of water, and stir to create a paste. Fry for 1–2 minutes.

3. Pour in the carlin peas and their bean stock, followed by the coconut milk. Crumble in the stock cube, if using, and stir in the spinach. Simmer for a few minutes until the mixture thickens slightly.

4. Transfer 2 ladlefuls of the mixture to a blender or food processor and blitz into a purée, then stir back into the pan – this will give it all a nice silky texture. If it's looking a little thick, add some water to loosen. Check for seasoning, bearing in mind that the halloumi will be salty, then leave to simmer, stirring occasionally, while you fry the halloumi.

5. Add the halloumi cubes and mango chutney to a small bowl and toss to coat. Heat a non-stick frying pan over a medium–high heat and cook the halloumi for 3–4 minutes, turning regularly, until golden all over. Add a splash of oil or water if it gets a little too sticky.

6. Once the curry has reached a creamy consistency, serve into bowls. Top with some kefir or yoghurt, if using, and scatter over the halloumi. Finish with the coriander leaves and a sprinkling of nigella seeds, if using. Serve with rice.

> **TOP TIP**
> For a vegan twist, simply swap the halloumi for tofu and use plant-based yoghurt.

CARLIN PEA STROGANOFF

Feeds 3–4
Takes 1 hour

This dish is the dictionary definition of heartwarming. The bean stock helps create a glossy sauce that's packed full of umami flavour from the mushrooms. Choose your carb accompaniment – mop up the leftovers with crusty bread, pour over silky mashed potatoes or spoon it over a big bowl of rice, baked potatoes or buttered tagliatelle.

500g (1lb 2oz) mixed mushrooms, *roughly sliced (we like chestnut, oyster and shiitake)*

2 tbsp olive oil

2 onions, *thinly sliced*

2 tsp fresh thyme leaves / 1 tsp dried thyme

1 tbsp tomato purée

2 tsp sweet paprika

½ tsp cayenne pepper

2 garlic cloves, *roughly chopped*

50ml (2fl oz) marsala wine or brandy

500ml (18fl oz) veg stock

2 tbsp crème fraîche or soured cream

1 tsp Dijon mustard

570g (1lb 4½oz) jarred carlin peas, *with their bean stock*

1 tbsp Worcestershire sauce or Henderson's Relish

15g (½oz) parsley, *finely chopped*

knob of butter *(optional)*

salt and pepper

TO SERVE

mashed potatoes, cooked rice, baked potatoes or buttered tagliatelle

steamed green beans *(optional)*

1. Start by dry-frying your mushrooms in a large, deep-sided casserole pan over a medium–high heat. Do this in two batches, first frying half of the mushrooms for about 5 minutes until coloured and crisping at the edges, then removing to a plate and repeating with the other half. Dry-frying gives them a bit more texture.

2. In the same pan, heat the olive oil over a medium–low heat. Add the onions, along with a pinch of salt, and cook gently for 20–25 minutes, stirring occasionally so that they don't catch. Cooking the onions slow like this will bring out a lovely caramelised flavour.

3. Add the thyme, tomato purée, sweet paprika, cayenne pepper and garlic to the onions and cook off for another 2 minutes until some of the onions start sticking to the bottom.

4. Deglaze the pan with the alcohol, then let it bubble off for a few minutes until it is reduced by half.

5. Now gradually add the stock, stirring the mixture to a smooth paste before adding more. Once all your stock is added, bring your mixture to a simmer for 2 minutes to thicken. Return the mushrooms to the pan, along with the crème fraîche, Dijon mustard and carlin peas, with their bean stock. Stir in the Worcestershire sauce or Henderson's Relish, along with most of the parsley. If using, swirl through a knob of butter to give it a bit more richness. Simmer for about 3 minutes more to warm it all through and ensure the mixture is creamy and glossy. Season with salt and lots of cracked black pepper.

6. Serve with the carb of your choice, topped with the remaining parsley, with some steamed green beans on the side, if you like.

TOP TIP

This one-pan recipe is ideal for batch cooking. Double up on all the ingredients, then freeze individual portions for a rainy day.

CARLIN PEA CAPRESE

Feeds 2 as a main, 4 as a side
Takes 40 minutes

When tomatoes are super ripe and in season, let them speak for themselves! Our version of a traditional caprese is elevated with our crisped-up, cacio e pepe-inspired carlin peas; sort of like a crouton, but beany and even more delicious. We love this as a main-character-energy side dish at a barbecue, or for a warm summer's evening dinner.

700g (1lb 9oz) jarred carlin peas, drained and rinsed

3 tbsp extra virgin olive oil

50g (1¾oz) Parmesan or vegetarian hard cheese, finely grated

1½ tsp cracked black pepper

650g (1lb 7oz) good-quality ripe tomatoes, roughly chopped

15g (½oz) basil leaves, torn

1 tsp red wine vinegar or balsamic vinegar

30g (1oz) pine nuts

125g (4½oz) buffalo mozzarella, torn

salt

1. Preheat the oven to 200°C/180°C fan/400°F/gas mark 6 and line a baking tray with baking paper.

2. Tumble the drained and rinsed carlin peas onto the prepared baking tray and pat dry with a clean tea towel or paper towels. Drizzle with 2 tablespoons of the olive oil and season with a good pinch of salt. Roast for 30 minutes. The moment they're out of the oven, add the grated Parmesan and black pepper and stir so the cheese melts on the hot tray. Leave to slightly cool – they will crisp up more as they're cooling.

3. Add the tomatoes to a bowl with the torn basil. Season, then dress with the remaining olive oil and the vinegar. Leave to sit for 15 minutes while the carlin peas crisp up.

4. Meanwhile, toast the pine nuts in a separate dry frying pan over a low heat for 2–3 minutes until golden.

5. To serve, toss the pine nuts and torn mozzarella through the tomatoes. Taste and season if needed. Plate up with the cacio e pepe carlin peas scattered on top.

TOP TIP

When choosing your tomatoes, try to find a mix of colours. They'll look very pretty with the soft torn mozzarella and scattering of vibrant basil.

ROASTED SQUASH WITH CREAMY MARMITE CARLINS + CRISPY SAGE

Feeds 4
Takes 1 hour 10 minutes

This veggie feast is autumn personified. Sweet and soft roasted hasselback squash, served alongside a creamy, cheesy gratin with crispy kale, with Marmite adding an umami kick to cut through the richness – what's not to love? To make it a feast, serve with honey-glazed roasted carrots and lemony, garlic greens.

---

1 large butternut squash (about 1kg/2lb 4oz), peeled, halved lengthways and seeds spooned out

5 tbsp olive oil

2 tsp dried oregano or thyme / 4 tsp fresh oregano or thyme leaves, roughly chopped

1 onion, thinly sliced

3 garlic cloves, crushed

2 tsp Marmite

570g (1lb 4½oz) jarred carlin peas, with their bean stock

250ml (9fl oz) double cream, or a plant-based alternative

10g (¼oz) sage leaves

150g (5½oz) Cheddar, grated

100g (3½oz) breadcrumbs

100g (3½oz) kale, woody stalks removed, sliced

1 tsp maple syrup or honey (optional)

salt and pepper

TO SERVE

honey-glazed roasted carrots

lemony, garlic wilted greens (we like Swiss chard, kale or spinach)

1. Preheat the oven to 200°C/180°C fan/400°F/gas mark 6 and line a baking tray with baking paper.

2. Place one squash half, cut-side down, on a chopping board. Slice into 1cm (½in) slices, but do not slide the knife all the way down. To help with this, place two chopsticks or wooden spoons along either side of the length of the squash. These will act as a cutting guide to prevent you slicing all the way through. Repeat with the other squash half.

3. Transfer each squash half, sliced side up, to the prepared baking sheet and drizzle with 2 tablespoons of the olive oil. Season, and scatter over the oregano or thyme. Roast for 50 minutes–1 hour, or until softened with a slightly golden top.

4. Meanwhile, heat 1 tablespoon of the olive oil in a large saucepan over a medium–low heat. Add the onion, season with salt, and cook for about 10 minutes until soft, stirring every now and then. Add the garlic and cook for a further minute, until fragrant. Add the Marmite, carlin peas and their bean stock, the cream and half the sage leaves, and simmer for about 5 minutes. Add two-thirds of the cheese and stir to melt before transferring into a deep baking dish.

5. Mix together the breadcrumbs and remaining cheese, and sprinkle in an even layer over the gratin. Bake for 10 minutes until the breadcrumbs are golden and the gratin is bubbling.

6. While this is baking, tumble the kale onto a roasting tray and toss with 1 tablespoon of the olive oil and a pinch of salt. Bake for 4–5 minutes until slightly crisp.

7. While everything is cooking, heat the remaining olive oil in a small frying pan over a medium heat and add the remaining sage leaves. Fry until slightly crisp – this will take about 1 minute. Transfer to a paper towel to remove any excess oil.

8. Remove the squash from the oven and drizzle over the maple syrup or honey, if using. Remove the gratin from the oven and scatter the crispy sage leaves over. Slide the squash onto a large serving platter and serve alongside a scoop of cheesy beans and crispy kale, and a generous helping of honey-glazed roasted carrots and lemony, garlic wilted greens.

CARLIN PEA PLOUGHMAN'S SALAD

Feeds 4
Takes 30 minutes

Carlin peas are British through and through, so they're the perfect bean to transform this classic pub staple into a fresh and vibrant salad. Like any good ploughman's, there are sweet, sour and funky flavours – and obviously the pickles are what make it stand out, made here with peppery radishes and mellow red onion.

---

2 thick slices of bread, *roughly torn into chunky croutons*
2 tbsp olive oil
700g (1lb 9oz) jarred carlin peas, *drained and rinsed*
2 little gem lettuces, *roughly chopped*
2 apples, *cored and thinly sliced*
200g (7oz) blue Stilton or mature Cheddar
salt and pepper

FOR THE PICKLED RADISHES AND ONION
200ml (7fl oz/⅓ pint) apple cider or white wine vinegar
100g (3½oz) caster sugar
10g (¼oz) fine sea salt
6 large radishes, *thinly sliced*
1 small red onion, *very thinly sliced*
100ml (3½fl oz) water

FOR THE DRESSING
4 tbsp extra virgin olive oil
2 tbsp apple cider or white wine vinegar
1 tsp English or Dijon mustard
1 tsp honey

1. Preheat the oven to 200°C/180°C fan/400°F/gas mark 6.

2. Begin by making the pickling liquor. Measure the vinegar, sugar and salt into a pan and bring to a boil. Stir, then remove from the heat. Place the radishes and red onion in a jar or bowl, pour over the hot pickling liquor, then top up with the measured water. Set aside for later. Leave to pickle for at least 30 minutes, but the longer you can pickle this for, the better!

3. For the croutons, place the torn bread on a baking tray, drizzle over the olive oil, season and mix everything together, ensuring the bread is nicely coated in the oil. Bake in the oven for 8–10 minutes, tossing halfway, until the bread is evenly crisp and golden.

4. Whisk all the dressing ingredients together in a salad bowl, and season to taste.

5. Add the carlin peas, lettuce, apples and croutons to the dressing bowl and toss to combine. Share between plates, then top with the pickled onion and radishes, and finish by crumbling over the cheese.

TOP TIP
If you eat meat, some sliced ham or crispy pancetta would be very tasty tumbled into this salad.

CRISPY BAKED HALLOUMI, CARLIN PEA + ORANGE SALAD

Feeds 2
Takes 30 minutes

This super easy lunch is a perfect antidote to sad desk salads. Think of it like an orange fattoush. It's light, refreshing and leaves you feeling FULL OF BEANS! You get a salty kick from the cheese, freshness from the herbs, sweetness from the oranges and crunch from the croutons. Plus it's a great way to use up old pittas or leftover bread.

225g (8oz) halloumi

2 pitta breads or leftover bread (optional)

2 tbsp olive oil

pinch of dried chilli flakes or chilli powder (optional)

25g (1oz) walnuts or pecans or almonds, roughly chopped

2 large oranges

570g (1lb 4½oz) jarred carlin peas, drained

15g (½oz) mint or dill, finely chopped

100g (3½oz) mixed salad leaves, such as rocket or spinach, roughly chopped

salt and pepper

FOR THE DRESSING

1 tsp Dijon mustard

1 tbsp honey

2 tsp apple cider vinegar or lemon juice

½ red bird's-eye chilli, deseeded and thinly sliced (optional)

2 tbsp extra virgin olive oil

1. Preheat the oven to 200°C/180°C fan/400°F/gas mark 6.

2. Tear the halloumi and pitta breads or leftover bread, if using, into rough bite-sized chunks. Tumble onto a baking tray and drizzle with the olive oil and chilli flakes, if using. Season, remembering that halloumi is already salty. Bake for 8 minutes, flipping halfway, then add the walnuts and bake for a further 3–5 minutes until everything is golden.

3. Meanwhile, prep the rest of the ingredients and make the dressing. Cut the peel and pith away from the oranges, then use a small serrated knife to segment them, catching any juices in a bowl. Set the segments aside. Squeeze any excess juice from the off-cut pith into the bowl as well. Use this as the base for your dressing: add the mustard, honey, vinegar or lemon juice, chilli, if using, and olive oil, then season with just a pinch of salt and pepper, and mix well to combine.

4. Add the drained carlin peas, mint, orange segments and salad leaves to a bowl, along with the crispy baked halloumi and walnuts.

5. When you're ready to eat, pour over the dressing and mix well, scatter over the croutons, then tip onto plates or a serving platter and serve.

TOP TIP

If you don't like mint, try using dill, basil or parsley. And if nuts aren't your thing, swap them for sunflower or pumpkin seeds.

FIVE-INGREDIENT TRAYBAKES

Sometimes, you want a bung-it-all-in dinner. One you don't have to think about, but that still delivers on flavour and makes you feel good.

These traybakes are for those moments. Each one is easy to pull together, uses only five ingredients (plus oil, salt and pepper) and, most importantly, tastes DELICIOUS!

Each traybake serves two, heartily.

HARISSA COD + WHITE BEANS

400g (14oz) pack of Mediterranean roasting veg (or similar)

2 cod fillets, skinless and boneless

1–2 tbsp harissa paste

570g (1lb 4½oz) jarred white beans, with their bean stock

handful of parsley, roughly choppped

1. Preheat your oven to 220°C/200°C fan/425°F/gas mark 7. Tip the Mediterranean roasting veg onto a roasting tray and drizzle with olive oil. Season, then spread out in a single layer on the tray and roast for 20 minutes. Meanwhile, season the cod fillets.

2. After 20 minutes, mix the harissa paste (depending on how spicy you like it) into the roasted veg, along with the white beans and their bean stock.

3. Once everything is mixed together, make two spaces in the middle of the tray to nestle in the cod fillets and drizzle over a little more oil. Return to the oven until the fish is cooked to your liking (we'd recommend around 8 minutes). Scatter over a handful of parsley and serve.

CHIPOTLE RED KIDNEY BEANS + BAKED FETA

3 red peppers, *cored, deseeded and thinly sliced*

2–3 tsp chipotle paste

½ × 570g (1lb 4½oz) jar red kidney beans, *with their bean stock*

250g (9oz) cooked rice

200g (7oz) feta

1. Preheat your oven 220°C/200°C fan/425°F/gas mark 7. Toss the peppers on a baking tray with some olive oil. Season, then spread into a single layer so that they roast evenly. Cook for 12–15 minutes until they start to soften.

2. Stir through the chipotle paste (depending on how spicy you like it), the red kidney beans with their bean stock and the cooked rice (you could use a microwaveable pack to make this easier).

3. Once well mixed, make space for the feta block in the middle of the tray. Drizzle with a little olive oil, then preheat the grill to high. Slide the tray under the grill for 5 minutes until the feta is golden on top and everything is heated through, then serve.

FIVE-INGREDIENT TRAYBAKES

FIVE-INGREDIENT TRAYBAKES continued

GARLICKY ZA'ATAR BLACK BEANS + TOMATOES

300g (10½oz) cherry tomatoes, *on the vine*

6 garlic cloves, *peeled and cut in half*

2 large slices of sourdough

570g (1lb 4½oz) jarred black beans, *with their bean stock*

1 tbsp za'atar

1. Preheat your oven to 180°C/160°C fan/350°F/gas mark 4. Take the cherry tomatoes off their vine (they're sweeter if you buy them on the vine) and place on a small baking tray. Add the halved garlic cloves, 4 tablespoons of olive oil and plenty of salt and pepper.

2. Cover in foil and roast for 25 minutes until the garlic is soft and the tomatoes are bursting. Remove the foil.

3. Brush 2 large slices of sourdough with some of the garlicky oil, then set aside. Add the black beans and their bean stock to the tray, along with the za'atar, and stir through the tomatoes and garlic.

4. Return the uncovered tray to the bottom of the oven and toast the bread on the racks above. Cook for a further 6–8 minutes, until the bread is toasted and the black beans are coated in the garlicky tomato sauce.

5. Serve the garlicky tomato beans on top of the toast with more za'atar sprinkled over.

CURRIED CHICKPEAS + PANEER

570g (1lb 4½oz) jarred chickpeas, *with their bean stock*

400ml (14fl oz) can coconut milk

2 tbsp + 2 tsp tikka masala curry paste

200g (7oz) sugar snap peas

225g (8oz) paneer, *cut into cubes*

1. Preheat your grill to medium–high. Tip the chickpeas and their bean stock into a baking tray, along with the coconut milk and 2 tablespoons of the tikka masala curry paste. Add the sugar snap peas and season.

2. In a separate bowl, mix another 2 teaspoons of the curry paste with 2 teaspoons of vegetable oil. Toss the paneer in the curried oil to make sure it's well coated, then add to the baking tray (making sure the paneer is on top).

3. Place the tray under the grill for 5–6 minutes until everything is nice and hot, and the veg and paneer have got a good colour on them.

4. Serve with yoghurt and a dollop of mango chutney for a bit of sweetness, if you like.

DATA SCIENTIST

"I CAN'T THINK OF A FOOD BETTER FOR THE PLANET THAN BEANS. IF YOU WANT TO EAT IN A CLIMATE-FRIENDLY AND ENVIRONMENTALLY FRIENDLY WAY, EATING MORE BEANS IS ONE OF THE BEST THINGS YOU CAN DO. EVEN THE 'LEAST SUSTAINABLE' BEANS HAVE A MUCH LOWER CARBON FOOTPRINT THAN THE 'BEST' MEAT AND DAIRY."

– Dr Hannah Ritchie

RED KIDNEY BEANS

Kidney beans are so underrated – we think they are sweet and melt-in-the-mouth delicious.

RAJMA KEBABS WITH LETTUCE CUPS, RAITA + CUMIN POTATOES

Feeds 4–6 (makes about 12 kebabs)
Takes 1 hour

 RINKU DUTT

There's nothing quite like a cooling raita with something hot and spicy. Here, Rinku Dutt has reimagined *rajma*, a North Indian dish traditionally packed with red kidney beans. 'I created rajma kebabs as a starter for one of my supper clubs, and they've been a hit ever since!' Green chilli brings heat, cashews lend creaminess and feta adds a salty kick.

---

1 tsp cumin seeds

570g (1lb 4½oz) jarred red kidney beans, *drained*

4 garlic cloves, *roughly chopped*

thumb-sized piece of fresh ginger, *roughly chopped*

small handful of mint leaves, *roughly chopped*

1 green chilli, *roughly chopped*

20g (¾oz) cashew nuts

100g (3½oz) feta, *roughly broken into chunks*

3 heaped tbsp fried onions *(shop-bought is fine)*

1 tsp ground black pepper

1 tsp ground cumin

1 tsp garam masala

5 heaped tbsp gram flour or plain flour, *plus a little extra if needed*

5 tbsp neutral oil, such as sunflower or rapeseed oil

salt and pepper

FOR THE RAITA

5 tbsp Greek or natural yoghurt

juice of 1 lemon

½ large cucumber, *halved lengthways, deseeded and finely chopped*

½ tsp fine sea salt

2 tsp mint sauce *(shop-bought is fine)*

small handful of mint leaves, *chopped*

1. Preheat the oven to 200°C/180°C fan/400°F/gas mark 6 and line a large baking sheet with baking parchment.

2. Put all the raita ingredients in a bowl and mix well. Check for seasoning and acidity, adjusting to your preference, then set aside in the refrigerator.

3. Now make the cumin-roasted potatoes. Parboil the potatoes for about 15 minutes in a large pan of simmering salted water until fork-tender. Drain, then tip onto the prepared baking sheet. Toss with the olive oil and cumin, season, then roast for 25–30 minutes until golden brown, turning halfway.

4. Meanwhile, in a small frying pan, carefully dry-roast the cumin seeds over a medium heat for 2–3 minutes. Take care not to burn them – remove from the heat as soon as the aromas are released. Set aside to cool.

5. Add the red kidney beans to a food processor and blitz until the mixture looks like a semi-smooth dough (a little texture is fine). Transfer to a large mixing bowl.

6. To the same food processor, add the remaining ingredients, apart from the flour and oil. Blend until smooth – some small chunks of cashew nuts are fine. If needed, add a little water, a splash at a time – don't add too much though, as the texture should be thick. Transfer to the mixing bowl and combine with the red bean mixture. Add the gram flour or plain flour gradually, mixing gently to ensure no lumps are left and that everything is well combined. The dough should be a little sticky, but not too wet. Add a little more flour if necessary.

7. Heat the oil in a frying pan over a medium heat, ready for shallow-frying. Once hot, carefully take a small amount of the red bean mixture in oiled hands and shape into a rough, sausage-like cylinder – they don't need to be too perfect. Carefully place the kebab into the hot oil. Continue shaping kebabs and adding them to the pan, leaving space between each one and taking care not to overfill the pan – work in batches, if necessary. Cook the kebabs for 3 minutes on each side until both sides are crispy and golden brown. Remove from the heat to a baking tray lined with paper towels. Allow to cool before serving.

FOR THE CUMIN-ROASTED POTATOES

1kg (2lb 4oz) potatoes *(we love Maris Piper), peeled and cut into small chunks*

2 tbsp olive oil

1 tbsp ground cumin

TO SERVE

4 little gem lettuces, *leaves separated*

8. To assemble the kebabs, line a serving plate with 12 lettuce cups and fill each cup with a rajma kebab. Add a dollop of raita – we like to add some pomegranate seeds and a few coriander leaves too. Dig in and enjoy along with the crispy cumin potatoes.

CRISPY CHORIZO + RED BEAN SHAKSHUKA WITH CHARRED PADRON PEPPERS

Feeds 2 as a main, or 4 as part of a brunch spread
Takes 45 minutes

We'd eat this for breakfast, lunch and dinner. Getting the chorizo really crispy and letting everything else take on the flavour is the real trick here. Try to find fresh cooking chorizo, as the spices and flavours will release more gradually as it cooks, and the softer texture means it will stay juicy and tender. This dish NEEDS a hunk of bread for dunking.

200g (7oz) cooking chorizo, sliced into 5mm (¼in) rounds

200g (7oz) padron peppers

1 tbsp olive oil

1 small red onion, finely chopped

1 garlic clove, finely chopped

2 tsp smoked paprika

1 tsp ground cumin

½ tsp chilli powder or cayenne pepper

400g (14oz) can chopped or cherry tomatoes

570g (1lb 4½oz) jarred red kidney beans, with their bean stock

pinch of white or brown sugar (optional)

4 eggs

15g (½oz) parsley, roughly chopped (optional)

flaky sea salt and pepper

TO SERVE

Tabasco (optional)

lemon wedges

crusty bread or toasted crumpets

1. Heat a large, high-sided frying pan over a medium–high heat. Add the chorizo and cook, stirring occasionally, for 5–6 minutes until browned and crispy, letting it release its smoky oils.

2. Remove the chorizo from the pan with a slotted spoon and set aside on a plate, leaving the oils in the pan. With the pan still on the heat, add the padron peppers and cook for 4–5 minutes, turning occasionally, until blistered and charred – you want them collapsing and browned on all sides. Remove from the pan, set aside on another plate and sprinkle with some flaky sea salt.

3. In the same pan, heat the olive oil, then add the onion, along with a pinch of salt. Cook for about 8 minutes until soft and fragrant. Add the garlic, smoked paprika, cumin and chilli powder or cayenne pepper, and cook for a few minutes more until mellowed and fragrant.

4. Add the chopped tomatoes and the red kidney beans with their bean stock, and mix to combine. Bubble away for 3–4 minutes with the lid on. Taste for seasoning, adding a pinch of sugar if needed, depending on the sharpness of your tomatoes.

5. Uncover the pan and make four wells in the sauce using the back of a spoon. Break in the eggs, nestling each egg in a well within the sauce. Cover the pan and cook on a low-medium heat for about 5 minutes, or until the egg whites have set but the yolks are still somewhat runny.

6. When the eggs are ready, scatter the crispy chorizo over the top, then sprinkle over the parsley, if using. Plonk in the middle of the table for people to self-serve, with the padron peppers alongside, and offer wedges of lemon, some Tabasco and crusty bread or toasted crumpets.

> **TOP TIP**
> *If you have some soft greens in the refrigerator, chuck them in with the chopped tomatoes to wilt in the sauce – kale works particularly well.*

RED KIDNEY BEANS

CHEESY BEAN BRUNCH HOTCAKES WITH MAPLE BACON

Feeds 4
Takes 40–45 minutes

These have a similar texture to fluffy American-style pancakes, but are cheesy, herby and beany, perfect for when you need a savoury kick in the morning. Stacked with whole red beans and packed with herby goodness, they pair perfectly with the maple-drenched bacon. Add a dollop of crème fraîche and serve in bed on a lazy weekend morning.

200g (7oz) streaky bacon, *chopped into bite-sized pieces*

1 tbsp maple syrup, *plus extra to serve*

100g (3½oz) self-raising flour

50g (1¾oz) mature Cheddar, *grated, plus extra for sprinkling*

10g (¼oz) parsley, *finely chopped*

1 spring onion, *roughly chopped*

10g (¼oz) fresh chives / 1 tsp dried chives, *finely chopped*

570g (1lb 4½oz) jarred red kidney beans, *drained and rinsed*

2 medium eggs

6 tbsp milk

2 tbsp olive oil

salt and pepper

TO SERVE
crème fraîche, soured cream or Greek yoghurt

4 poached eggs *(optional)*

1. Preheat the oven to 220°C/200°C fan/425°F/gas mark 7 and line a baking tray with baking parchment.

2. Scatter the chopped bacon over the prepared tray and brush with the maple syrup. Top with another piece of baking paper and place a second baking tray on top to weigh it down. Bake for 15–20 minutes until the bacon is sticky and browned. Set aside to cool slightly.

3. In a large bowl, mix together the flour, cheese, parsley, spring onions and most of the chives (saving some for garnish). Add the red kidney beans and season with salt and pepper. Tip a third of the maple bacon pieces into the bowl, then make a well in the centre and break in the eggs. Beat with a wooden spoon, then gradually add the milk, drawing the flour into the centre as you go. You should end up with a fairly thick batter.

4. Heat the olive oil in a frying pan over a medium heat and, once hot, drop in large spoonfuls of the batter, making sure not to overcrowd the pan. Depending on the size of your pan, you should be able to cook several hotcakes at once. Sprinkle a little Cheddar on the top (raw) sides of the hotcakes, and cook for 3–4 minutes until the hotcakes start to set around the edges and turn golden. Carefully flip them over, then cook on the other side for another 3–4 minutes until golden. You'll need to do this in batches, so keep the cooked hot cakes under a tea towel to keep warm while you cook the rest.

5. Serve each person 2 hotcakes, topped with a dollop of crème fraîche, scattered with the remaining chives and maple bacon. Finish with an extra drizzle of maple syrup. Add a poached egg, too, if you fancy!

TOP TIP
Use plant-based bacon (adjust the cooking timings according to the packet instructions) and milk for a just-as-delicious veggie version.

'NDUJA BEANS, MOZZARELLA + HOT HONEY

Feeds 2–3
Takes 20 minutes

'Nduja is a delicious, cured and spreadable spiced sausage from Calabria. A hint of this heat with melting beans, cool, creamy mozzarella and crunchy breadcrumbs, and you have a super-simple dish ready in just 20 minutes – delicious morning, noon and night. To make your own hot honey, simply mix honey with a few dried chilli flakes.

---

2 tbsp olive oil
1 onion, sliced
2 garlic cloves, thinly sliced
1 tbsp tomato purée
1 tsp dried oregano
400g (14oz) can good-quality chopped tomatoes
570g (1lb 4½oz) jarred red kidney beans, with their bean stock
100g (3½oz) cavolo nero or kale, tough stems removed, roughly chopped
125g (4½oz) mozzarella, torn into small pieces
1–2 tbsp 'nduja paste
20g (¾oz) breadcrumbs
2–3 tsp honey or hot honey
salt and pepper

TO SERVE (OPTIONAL)
warm ciabatta or sourdough
salad leaves

1. Heat the olive oil in an ovenproof frying pan over a medium heat. Once hot, tip in the onion and cook for 8–10 minutes until softened, then add the garlic and tomato purée and fry off, stirring, for a further 2 minutes.

2. Add the oregano, chopped tomatoes and red kidney beans with their bean stock. Stir to combine, then bubble away for 2–3 minutes to let the mixture thicken slightly. Now add the cavolo nero or kale, and cook for 2–3 minutes more until wilted. Season to taste.

3. Preheat the grill to medium–high.

4. Scatter the torn mozzarella evenly over the beans, dot over small pieces of the 'nduja, and cover the top with breadcrumbs. Transfer the pan to the grill for 1–2 minutes, or until the breadcrumbs are golden, the mozzarella is oozing and the 'nduja is cooked through. Remove from the grill and drizzle over the honey or hot honey.

5. Scoop the mixture from the pan onto plates, or just plonk in the centre of the table for people to help themselves. Serve with warm, crusty bread and a fresh salad, if you like.

TOP TIP

To make a veggie version, we recommend using a sun-dried tomato paste, because it delivers the same tomatoey brightness – add some chilli flakes for that extra kick of heat.

SMOKY CHILLI WITH FLUFFY SWEETCORN DUMPLINGS

Feeds 4–6
Takes 1 hour 15 minutes

Although our plump, jewel-toned red beans are the star of the dish, this is not your average chilli. We've deployed a secret-weapon ingredient – harissa paste, for a spicy, smoky hit – and reimagined the usual accompaniments to include a crispy yet light and fluffy dumpling crust. It's THE perfect warming dish for a snuggly Sunday on the sofa.

2 tbsp olive oil

1 red or brown onion, *finely diced*

1 large celery stalk, *finely diced*

2 carrots, *finely diced*

1 red pepper, *cored, deseeded and finely diced*

3 garlic cloves, *crushed*

2 tsp smoked paprika

1 tsp ground cumin

½ tsp dried chilli flakes

2 tbsp tomato purée

1 tbsp harissa paste

570g (1lb 4½oz) jarred red kidney beans, *with their bean stock*

400g (14oz) chopped tomatoes

10g (¼oz) dark chocolate *(about 1 square)*

salt and pepper

green salad or steamed broccoli, *to serve*

FOR THE DUMPLINGS

300g (10½oz) self-raising flour

1 tsp bicarbonate of soda

160g (5¾oz) butter, *cold and cubed*

100g (3½oz) mature Cheddar, *grated*

285g (10¼oz) canned sweetcorn, *drained*

20g (¾oz) chives, *finely chopped*

250ml (9fl oz) milk

1. Preheat the oven to 200°C/180°C fan/400°F/gas mark 6.

2. Heat the olive oil in a large frying pan over a low–medium heat. Add the onion, celery and carrots, and fry for about 15 minutes until starting to soften. Add the red pepper and garlic, and continue to cook for 5 minutes.

3. Add the smoked paprika, cumin, chilli flakes, tomato purée, harissa paste and a pinch of salt. Cook for a further 3 minutes, stirring occasionally, before adding in the red kidney beans (along with their bean stock), tomatoes and chocolate. Stir to combine, then allow to simmer while you make the dumpling mix.

4. For the dumplings, tip the flour, bicarbonate of soda and a pinch of salt into a large mixing bowl. Add the cold cubed butter, and rub the flour and butter together between your thumb and fingers until you are left with a breadcrumb texture and no large lumps of butter.

5. Tip in the Cheddar, sweetcorn and chives, and mix to incorporate. Pour in the milk and mix with a wooden spoon until a thick, sticky batter forms.

6. Carefully pour the chilli mixture into a large, deep baking dish. Spoon the corn dumpling mix over the chilli in an even layer. It is easiest to do this by placing small spoonfuls over the chilli to create one layer.

7. Bake in the oven for 30 minutes until the dumpling layer is golden and crispy, then serve with a green salad or some steamed broccoli.

TOP TIP

To save time, or if you are cooking for veg-phobic children, blitz up the onion, carrot and celery in a food processor until super finely chopped.

SMOKY KIMCHI BEANS WITH CRISPY TEMPEH CRUMB

Feeds 2, or 4 with rice
Takes 40 minutes

XUXA MILROSE

Gochujang is a Korean spice paste that adds depth and a big hit of spicy smokiness here to soft, creamy beans. This dish was dreamed up by Xuxa Milrose, a nutritional therapist who is all about supporting gut health, immunity and mood. 'This recipe combines my love for beans, kimchi and a mix of textures, including crispy tempeh!'

---

1 tbsp olive oil
1 large onion, finely diced
4 garlic cloves, crushed
1 tbsp tomato purée
2 tsp smoked paprika
1 tbsp gochujang or chilli paste (use less if you're not so keen on spice)
2 tbsp soy sauce
570g (1lb 4½oz) jarred red kidney beans, with their bean stock
1 tbsp maple syrup
400g (14oz) can chopped tomatoes
150g (5½oz) spinach
200g (7oz) kimchi, roughly chopped, plus a little extra to serve
2–4 eggs (optional)

FOR THE TEMPEH
1 tbsp olive oil
1 tbsp maple syrup
1 tbsp soy sauce
1 tsp garlic powder
2 tsp smoked paprika
pinch of salt
200g (7oz) tempeh

TO SERVE
3 spring onions, chopped
sesame seeds, for sprinkling
coriander leaves (optional)
cooked rice (optional)

1. Put all the tempeh marinade ingredients into a shallow bowl and mix to combine. Roughly crumble in the tempeh, making sure it is fully submerged and well coated. Transfer to the refrigerator and leave to marinate for at least 30 minutes. (The longer the better, ideally. This is a great one to do in the morning before work.)

2. When you're ready to cook, preheat the oven to 200°C/180°C fan/400°F/gas mark 6 and line a baking tray with baking paper. Tip the tempeh onto the prepared tray and bake for 8–10 minutes or until evenly crisp, flipping halfway through.

3. Meanwhile, heat the olive oil in a saucepan over a medium heat. Tip in the onion and cook for 8–10 minutes, stirring regularly, until translucent. Then add the garlic and cook for 1 minute more. Add the tomato purée and smoked paprika, and cook, stirring, for 1–2 minutes before adding the gochujang or chilli paste and soy sauce. Stir well and cook for another 2 minutes.

4. Pour in the red kidney beans and their bean stock, stir thoroughly, then add the maple syrup and chopped tomatoes. Add a splash of water to the tomato can and swill it around, then add that to the pan too. Reduce the heat to medium–low and cook for about 10 minutes until reduced. Chuck in the spinach and let that wilt down. You can add the kimchi now if you like but, if you want to maximise the health benefits, do this at the very last minute to keep the bacteria live!

5. If you're serving this with eggs (you'll need 1 per person), bring a saucepan of water to the boil. Carefully lower the eggs into the pan and cook for 5–6 minutes, then drain, rinse under cold water and peel.

6. Once the tempeh is cooked and crispy, let it cool for a couple of minutes, then crumble into smaller pieces.

7. Serve the beans topped with the crumbled tempeh, along with the soft-boiled eggs, if using. Sprinkle over the spring onions, sesame seeds and coriander, if using. Serve with rice if you fancy a heartier meal.

MEDITERRANEAN COD, CHORIZO + RED BEAN STEW

Feeds 2–3
Takes 40 minutes

There's something about the way the chorizo releases its paprika-spiced oil when cooked down, mixed with flaky cod and creamy red beans here, that just makes sense. This Mediterranean-inspired recipe packs in loads of veggies, gently spiced with paprika and a little cayenne kick to complement the chorizo.

---

2 tbsp olive oil

1 onion, roughly chopped

2 large garlic cloves, finely sliced

100g (3½oz) chorizo or cooking chorizo, chopped into small chunks

1 small courgette, diced

½ red pepper, cored, deseeded and roughly chopped

1 tbsp sweet smoked paprika

½ tsp cayenne pepper or dried chilli flakes

400g (14oz) can good-quality chopped tomatoes

pinch of white or brown sugar (optional)

570g (1lb 4½oz) jarred red kidney beans, with their bean stock

3 cod fillets, about 175–225g (6–8oz) each (or 1 per person)

handful of parsley, finely chopped

juice of ½ lemon, plus wedges to serve

salt and pepper

1. Heat the olive oil in a large, high-sided frying pan over a medium heat. Once hot, add the onion, along with a pinch of salt, and cook for 8–10 minutes until softened.

2. Add the garlic and fry for a further minute until fragrant, then add the chopped chorizo and fry for about 5 minutes, stirring occasionally, until the oils start to release.

3. Throw in the courgette, red pepper, sweet smoked paprika and cayenne pepper, then toss to coat everything in the oils. Cook for 5–6 minutes until the vegetables are starting to soften.

4. Stir in the chopped tomatoes. If your tomatoes are quite sour (tip: fancier brands are sweeter), add the sugar now. Bring to a boil, then reduce to a simmer for a couple of minutes to allow the sauce to thicken slightly.

5. Pour in the red kidney beans with their bean stock, then stir to combine and bubble away for 2–3 minutes to warm the beans through and allow the mixture to thicken slightly. Check for seasoning and adjust to taste.

6. Nestle the cod fillets on top of the stew and season with a pinch of salt and a grind of pepper. Cover with a lid and gently simmer over a low–medium heat for 8–10 minutes, or until the cod is fully cooked through. It should flake easily.

7. Scatter over the parsley and squeeze over the lemon juice. Serve into bowls with lemon wedges.

> **TOP TIP**
> *If you like, you can offer some crusty bread for dunking as well – perfect for soaking up all that flavour at the bottom!*

WHIPPED RED BEANS + CRISPY RICE SALAD

Feeds 2
Takes 20 minutes

Bold Bean enthusiast Catherine Sarsfield wanted to find a different way of incorporating red beans into salads, to deliver little bombs of texture and flavour in every bite. Whipped into pink clouds and layered underneath a salad dressed with a lime-miso vinaigrette and studded with crispy rice, the beans offer up the perfect amount of creaminess.

small knob of butter

½ tbsp olive oil

250g (9oz) cooked white rice or wild rice

handful of kale, *tough stalks removed, leaves shredded*

¼ × 570g (1lb 4½oz) jar red kidney beans, *drained and rinsed*

½ head of red cabbage, *thinly sliced and diced*

½ cucumber, *sliced into matchsticks*

handful of parsley, coriander or dill, *finely chopped*

50g (1¾oz) feta *(optional)*

salt and pepper

FOR THE WHIPPED RED BEANS

½ × 570g (1lb 4½oz) jar red kidney beans, *drained*

1 tbsp tahini

2 tbsp Greek yoghurt

juice of ½ lime

FOR THE LIME-MISO VINAIGRETTE

zest and juice of ½ lime

1 tbsp white or red miso

1 tbsp maple syrup

1 garlic clove, *grated*

large thumb-sized piece of fresh ginger, *grated*

2 tbsp sesame oil

1. In a blender, whiz together all the ingredients for the whipped beans. Blitz until smooth (you're looking for a thick consistency), then season to taste. Set aside.

2. In a large frying pan, melt the butter and olive oil over a medium heat. Once foaming, add the rice and cook for 8–10 minutes, until it's crisped up and starting to char (if the rice breaks up into clusters, that's fine). Make sure to flip the rice now and then to ensure it is evenly crisp and golden. Once nice and crispy, tip the rice out into a bowl.

3. Meanwhile, put all the ingredients for the vinaigrette in a large mixing bowl and mix well to combine. Add the kale, and use your hands to massage the dressing into the leaves to soften them slightly. Toss through the red kidney beans, along with the cabbage, cucumber, herbs, crispy rice and feta, if using.

4. Spread the whipped beans onto a serving plate and spoon the crispy rice salad on top.

TOP TIP

This recipe uses three-quarters of a 570g (1lb 4½oz) jar of red beans – add the rest to a tomatoey veggie curry for a bit of creamy bulk.

BEETROOT, RED BEAN + MACKEREL SALAD

Feeds 2–3
Takes 5 minutes

Creamy red beans enhance this classic combination of salty smoked mackerel and earthy beetroot, balanced with tangy crème fraîche. It takes five minutes to prep, which by our accounts makes it one of the fastest and tastiest lunches you can whip up when you're in need of something substantial, satisfying and, of course, DELICIOUS.

250g (9oz) vacuum-packed cooked beetroot, *chopped into bite-sized chunks*

2 celery stalks, *finely sliced*

50g (1¾oz) roasted mixed nuts or cashews, *roughly chopped*

1 cucumber, *peeled into ribbons and core chopped*

570g (1lb 4½oz) jarred red kidney beans, *drained and rinsed*

280g (10oz) smoked mackerel fillets *(we like peppered smoked mackerel fillets)*

2 tbsp lemon juice

salt and pepper

FOR THE DRESSING

2 tbsp crème fraîche or Greek yoghurt

2 tsp wholegrain or Dijon mustard

zest and juice of ½ lemon

15g (½oz) dill, *three-quarters roughly chopped, remaining fronds left whole*

extra virgin olive oil, *if needed*

1. Put all the dressing ingredients, except the whole dill fronds, into a large mixing bowl and mix well to combine. If you prefer a runnier dressing, you can add a splash of water or extra virgin olive oil to loosen. Season with plenty of salt and cracked black pepper to taste. Check for acidity, adding more lemon juice, if you like.

2. To the same bowl, add the beetroot, celery, nuts, cucumber core and drained red kidney beans, and mix well to combine. Roughly flake in the mackerel and gently fold through, ensuring everything is coated in the dressing.

3. In a separate bowl, dress the cucumber ribbons in the lemon juice and season with black pepper.

4. Divide the salad between plates and serve straight away, topped with the cucumber ribbons and dill fronds.

> **TOP TIP**
> *If you like pickles, a few cornichons chopped into this salad would be great, or even a few pickled beetroots to cut through the mackerel.*

BEANS IN PASTA SAUCE

Serving beans in sauces traditionally associated with pasta is our all-time favourite way to convince even the most determined bean-sceptic to try our beans.

Beans are starchy and brilliant absorbers of flavour, so they act much like pasta in these dishes, but they're healthier for you, and for the planet. Each recipe here feeds 3 people and takes less than 30 minutes.

CHOOSE YOUR SAUCE

1. We like to choose sauces with great texture. As beans are more tender than al dente pasta, adding texture with your sauce is KEY.

CHOOSE YOUR BEAN

2. Big beans, like our Queen Chickpeas or Queen Butter Beans, really come into their own here as they add great texture to the dish. If you only have smaller beans to hand, that's not a problem, but you may want to add some crunchy croutons, crispy kale or nuts for that all-important texture variation.

TOMATO + MASCARPONE

300g (10½oz) cherry tomatoes

3 garlic cloves, *peeled*

2 tbsp olive oil

small pinch of dried chilli flakes

75g (2¾oz) mascarpone

570g (1lb 4½oz) jarred beans of your choice, *with their bean stock*

big handful of basil leaves

1. In a saucepan, mix the tomatoes and garlic with the olive oil and chilli flakes. Season, then cover and cook over a medium heat for 20 minutes until the garlic is soft and the tomatoes are bursting.

2. Break up the tomatoes and garlic with the back of a spoon and stir in the mascarpone. Add the beans with their bean stock and warm through for 2–3 minutes. Finish with a big handful of basil leaves and some grated Parmesan or vegetarian hard cheese, if you like.

CREAMY PEA PESTO

570g (1lb 4½oz) jarred beans of your choice, *with their bean stock*

200g (7oz) frozen peas, *thawed*

200g (7oz) cottage cheese

20g (¾oz) basil, *leaves picked*

1 garlic clove, *roughly chopped*

30g (1oz) Parmesan or vegetarian hard cheese

2 tbsp extra virgin olive oil

1. Tip the beans and their bean stock into a saucepan over a low heat. Leave to warm through while you add half the peas to a blender, along with the cottage cheese, basil leaves, garlic, Parmesan and olive oil.

2. Blend until smooth and season to taste.

3. Add the pea pesto and the remaining peas to the beans, and warm through for around 3 minutes. If you want, you can finish the dish with a squeeze of lemon juice and some crispy bacon bits.

BEANS IN PASTA SAUCE

BEANS IN PASTA SAUCE continued

CREAMY SAUSAGE + FENNEL

2 tbsp extra virgin olive oil

1 tsp fennel seeds

1 large fennel bulb, trimmed, cored, and chopped

1 onion, roughly chopped

3 garlic cloves, crushed

570g (1lb 4½oz) jarred beans of your choice, with their bean stock (we highly recommend butter beans)

3 tbsp mascarpone

450g (1lb) cooked sausages, chopped into bite-sized pieces

small bunch of parsley, chopped

30g (1oz) pecorino or vegetarian hard cheese, grated

2 tbsp lemon juice

1. Heat the olive oil in a large saucepan over a low heat. Add the fennel seeds and cook until fragrant, then add the chopped fennel, onion and garlic. Season with a pinch of salt and cook for 10–15 minutes until translucent.

2. Add the beans and their bean stock, along with the mascarpone. Fold through the sausage and finish with the parsley, grated cheese and a squeeze of lemon juice.

AGLIO E OLIO BEANS

5 tbsp olive oil, *plus extra to serve*

5 large garlic cloves, *finely sliced*

½–1 tsp dried chilli flakes

1 small head of broccoli, *florets coarsely grated, stems finely chopped*

570g (1lb 4½oz) jarred beans of your choice, *with their bean stock (chickpeas work best!)*

30g (1oz) parsley, *finely chopped*

40g (1½oz) Parmesan or vegetarian hard cheese, *grated (optional)*

juice of 1 lemon, *plus wedges to serve*

1. Heat the olive oil in a large saucepan over a low–medium heat. Add the garlic and chilli flakes (depending on how spicy you like it) and cook for 3 minutes until soft and translucent but not browned.

2. Add the grated broccoli florets and chopped stalks, along with a pinch of salt, and stir to coat in the oil. Tip in the beans with their bean stock. Swill the jar with a splash of water and pour that in too. Stir to coat.

3. Increase the heat to medium and cook for about 10 minutes, allowing the mixture to bubble and reduce until the bean stock and olive oil have emulsified into a thick, rich sauce.

4. Add most of the parsley, reserving some for a garnish, along with the grated Parmesan, if using, and the lemon juice. Season well to taste.

5. Divide between plates, then scatter over the remaining parsley. Finish with a drizzle of olive oil and another squeeze of lemon juice, if you like.

NUTRITIONIST

"BEANS ARE SUCH A SIMPLE JOY. THEY'RE FILLING, NOURISHING AND ENDLESSLY VERSATILE – PROOF THAT HEALTHY FOOD DOESN'T HAVE TO BE COMPLICATED. THEY'VE BEEN A STAPLE FOR GENERATIONS, QUIETLY DOING THEIR JOB OF BRINGING COMFORT AND GOODNESS TO THE TABLE. FOR ME, BEANS ARE ABOUT SLOWING DOWN, ENJOYING REAL FOOD, AND FEELING GOOD INSIDE AND OUT."

– Emily English

WHITE BEANS

We love these OG beans in dips, mashes and stews, where they can become the real hero of the dish. Creamy and mild, they soak up flavours incredibly well.

COSY CHICKEN + WHITE BEAN SOUP WITH CRISPY CHICKEN-SKIN CROUTONS

Feeds 4
Takes 45 minutes

Think of this as a soup for the soul. It's made using leftover roast chicken — save some of the skin for the crispy chicken-skin topping! The soup features two types of stock — chicken stock AND bean stock — creating layers of flavour. It's super fragrant with fresh and dried herbs, and the milk addition is an old Italian trick to keep things creamy.

250g (9oz) leftover roast chicken, shredded, skin reserved for the crispy topping

3 tbsp olive oil, plus extra to serve

1 onion, diced

1 carrot, diced

1 celery stalk, diced

2 garlic cloves, finely chopped

1–2 rosemary sprigs, leaves picked and chopped

1 tsp dried oregano or thyme

100g (3½oz) kale, chard or cavolo nero, roughly chopped

750ml (25fl oz) chicken stock

250ml (9fl oz) milk

570g (1lb 4½oz) jarred white beans, with their bean stock

1 bay leaf (optional)

salt and pepper

lemon wedges, to serve

1. If you have any leftover chicken skin from your roast that's gone all cold and flabby, this is the moment to turn it into something the table will be fighting for. Peel it off the chicken and heat a deep, heavy-bottomed saucepan over a medium–high heat (you don't want the hob too hot or you'll risk burning the chicken skin). Add 1 tablespoon of the olive oil, then lay the chicken skin in the pan in a single layer. Fry for 3–4 minutes on each side, moving the pieces around so they crisp up evenly. Once crisp, remove them using tongs and transfer to a plate lined with paper towels. Leave all the rendered fat in the pan to start your chicken soup.

2. Add the remaining oil to the pan (use a bit less if you had lots of chicken fat), reduce the heat a little and chuck in the onion, carrot and celery. Season, stir to coat the veggies in the oil, then gently cook for 15 minutes to soften.

3. Chuck in the garlic, rosemary and oregano, and cook for a further few minutes, then add the chicken and kale, and stir everything together. Season again, then pour in the chicken stock and milk. Add the beans with their bean stock, and bring to a simmer. Add a bay leaf at this point, too, if you like. Cook for 10–12 minutes.

4. Divide between deep bowls, then top with an extra splash of olive oil and a handful of the crispy chicken skin. Serve with lemon wedges on the side for squeezing over.

TOP TIP

To make your own stock, simmer the leftover roast chicken carcass in 2 litres (3½ pints) of water, with some chopped carrots, celery, onion and herbs, for 3 hours. Drain before using.

WATERCRESS + WHITE BEAN SOUP WITH CHARRED ASPARAGUS

Feeds 3
Takes 20 minutes

This soup screams spring – loaded with creamy white beans and fresh, peppery watercress. The base is super simple to make and ends up a vivid, vibrant green colour. Add a dollop of yoghurt, and you have a banging lunch ready to go. To pimp it up a little, we've added seasonal asparagus tips and toasted pine nuts for extra crunch.

---

2 tbsp extra virgin olive oil

1 onion or 2 banana shallots, *chopped*

2 fat garlic cloves, *crushed*

570g (1lb 4½oz) jarred white beans, *with their bean stock*

300ml (10fl oz/½ pint) veg stock

100g (3½oz) watercress *(or use a mixed watercress, spinach and rocket salad bag)*

200g (7oz) asparagus tips, *cut into 2.5cm (1in) pieces*

20g (¾oz) pine nuts or pumpkin seeds

150g (5½oz) natural yoghurt or kefir

salt and pepper

drizzle of chilli oil, *to serve (optional)*

1. Heat 1 tablespoon of the oil in a medium saucepan over a low–medium heat. Add the onion or shallots and cook slowly, stirring occasionally, for around 10 minutes until softened. Season, add the garlic and cook for 1 minute more.

2. Tip in the beans, along with their bean stock, then add the veg stock and watercress. Simmer for a few minutes to allow the beans to warm through and the watercress to wilt. Using a handheld blender, blitz until you reach a creamy consistency, adding a splash of water or extra stock to loosen if necessary. (If you don't have a handheld blender, allow to cool, then blitz in a food processor or blender, then warm gently to reheat.) Season to taste. Keep the soup warm over a low heat while you fry the asparagus.

3. Drizzle the remaining olive oil into a frying pan over a high heat. Add the asparagus, and fry, stirring occasionally, for 3–4 minutes until tender and vivid green in colour.

4. Meanwhile, toast the pine nuts or pumpkin seeds in a separate dry frying pan over a low heat for 2–3 minutes until golden.

5. Divide the soup between bowls, then top with the yoghurt, asparagus, toasted pine nuts or seeds and a drizzle of chilli oil, if you like, for a little kick.

> **TOP TIP**
> *It's easy to make a vegan version of this delicious soup – simply replace the yoghurt with your favourite plant-based yoghurt.*

CRISPY WHITE BEANS + SAGE-FRIED EGGS WITH GARLICKY GREENS

Feeds 2
Takes 25 minutes

Garlicky greens and fried eggs are a great combo, but adding white beans brings a whole new level of deliciousness. We usually love to add some bean stock to our recipes, but not this time – you need the beans to crisp up and create a delicious bed for the fried eggs to nestle into. Don't skimp on the fried sage – it smells, and tastes, heavenly!

---

3 tbsp olive oil

570g (1lb 4½oz) jarred white beans, *drained, rinsed and patted dry with a paper towel*

1 tbsp butter

small bunch of sage, *leaves picked*

2 garlic cloves, *thinly sliced*

100g (3½oz) leafy greens, such as kale, spinach, chard or cavolo nero, *roughly chopped*

zest and juice of 1 lemon

2–4 eggs, *depending on hunger*

pinch of dried chilli flakes *(optional)*

salt and pepper

1. Heat 2 tablespoons of the oil in a large frying pan over a high heat. Tip in the beans and stir to coat in the oil, then spread them out so that they form a single layer across the base of the pan. Cover and leave undisturbed for 3–4 minutes so that one side can get nice and crispy. Stir, then cook for another 3–4 minutes until starting to turn brown. Some of the beans will break up, but that's fine.

2. Meanwhile, melt the butter in a separate frying pan over a medium-high heat. Fry the sage leaves until they turn dark green and slightly crisp – about 30 seconds–1 minute. Remove from the pan and set aside in a bowl. Add the remaining oil to the pan if needed, and fry the garlic, chopped greens and a pinch of salt for 2–4 minutes until the greens are just wilted but still vibrant, stirring frequently. Finish with half of the lemon juice.

3. Make small holes in the middle of the beans for the eggs – these holes don't need to be completely empty of beans, it's just about creating some space so the eggs can cook better. Now crack the eggs into the spaces in the beans, moving the pan to get the whites into as many of the crevices as you can. Increase the heat to high and fry until the whites are set and crispy, but the yolks are still runny (or cooked to your liking). If you're worried about the beans overcooking, cover the pan with a lid to speed up the egg whites. Season with salt, pepper and a pinch of chilli flakes, if you like, and scatter the fried sage leaves on top.

4. Plate up the crispy beans and eggs using a spatula to get all the banging crispy bits off the bottom of the pan. Scatter with the lemon zest and serve alongside the wilted greens, with the rest of the lemon juice squeezed on top, if you like.

TONNATO BEANS WITH TOMATOES + CAPERS

Feeds 4 as a starter or 2 as a light main
Takes 15 minutes

We just love tonnato, a classic recipe that whizzes up tuna, garlic, mayo and anchovies to create a luxurious sauce. We've swapped out the mayo for our white beans, which keep it creamy in the most delicious, beany way, and topped it with juicy tomatoes, crunchy red onion and tart, salty capers. It's a decadent dish that still leaves you feeling GREAT.

570g (1lb 4½oz) jarred white beans, with their bean stock

160g (5¾oz) canned tuna in olive oil

2 anchovy fillets

2 tsp Dijon mustard

1 garlic clove, peeled

juice of 1 lemon

1–3 tbsp extra virgin olive oil

1 small red onion, finely chopped

200g (7oz) high-quality tomatoes, roughly chopped into bite-sized pieces

2 tbsp capers, rinsed

15g (½oz) parsley or basil leaves, roughly chopped

sourdough crackers, to serve

1. To make the sauce, tip half of the beans and their bean stock into a food processor. Add the tuna with its oil, along with the anchovies, mustard and garlic. Squeeze in half the lemon juice and blend until smooth and creamy. Top up with 1–2 tablespoons of the olive oil, then season to taste. If the sauce is too thick, add a little water to loosen it. Set aside.

2. In a bowl, combine the red onion, tomatoes, capers and herbs, along with the remaining lemon juice and 1 tablespoon of the olive oil. Season, toss well, then let the mixture sit and marinate for a few minutes.

3. Tip the remaining white beans into a colander and rinse with fresh water to remove the sticky stock.

4. Once you're ready to assemble, spread the tonnato sauce over a large serving plate or platter. Scatter the remaining white beans on top for added texture. Spoon the marinated tomato-and-caper mixture over the beans, allowing some of the juices to drizzle onto the tonnato. Sprinkle with fresh basil or parsley, top with an extra drizzle of olive oil and serve immediately, with crackers for dunking.

TOP TIP

For something slightly sweeter, swap the tomatoes for 100g (3½oz) sun-ripened tomatoes – the ones found in plastic tubs in the antipasti aisle of the supermarket.

WHITE BEANS + CHARRED CABBAGE WITH CAPER + PARSLEY VINAIGRETTE

Feeds 4
Takes 30–35 minutes

We all know that charred cabbage is a thing of beauty, but we've taken it one step further, nestling the wedges into garlicky white beans for the ultimate veggie comfort food. Then there is the zesty lemon, caper and parsley dressing, which sets it off perfectly. Hearty, veggie goodness that makes you feel fancy.

---

5 tbsp olive oil

2 small savoy or sweetheart cabbages, quartered lengthways into wedges, stems kept intact

1 onion, roughly chopped

3 fat garlic cloves, crushed

570g (1lb 4½oz) jarred white beans, with their bean stock

zest of 1 lemon

salt and pepper

FOR THE DRESSING

3 tbsp capers, roughly chopped

15g (½oz) parsley, finely chopped

4 tbsp lemon juice

4 tbsp olive oil

25g (1oz) Parmesan or vegetarian hard cheese, grated, plus extra to serve

1. Heat your largest non-stick frying pan, for which you have a lid, over a medium–high heat, and add 3 tablespoons of the olive oil. Season the cabbages all over and place them into the pan, cut-side down. Cook for 2–3 minutes, moving them around a little as they cook. Once the bottom has a lovely golden brown colour, flip on to the other cut side and cook for the same amount of time. Once both sides of each piece are deeply golden, remove and set aside on a plate.

2. In the same pan, heat the remaining olive oil over a medium heat. Tip in the onion and cook for 7–8 minutes until starting to soften and caramelise. Add the garlic and cook for another minute until fragrant.

3. Add the beans to the pan with their bean stock, and mix well to combine. Reduce the heat slightly and add half of the lemon zest. Season generously with cracked black pepper.

4. Add the cabbage quarters to the pan, cover with the lid, and simmer for 6–8 minutes until the cabbage is lovely and tender.

5. While everything's cooking, combine all the dressing ingredients in a small bowl, then mix well and season with some cracked black pepper. (Alternatively, add them to your empty bean jar – no need to wash it out, as the starchy stock is delicious – and give it a good shake.) Add more olive oil to loosen, if necessary.

6. Finish by drizzling over the chunky dressing, then top with the remaining lemon zest and some extra Parmesan. Put the pan in the middle of the table for everyone to help themselves.

SPRING GREEN BEANOTTO

Feeds 2–3
Takes 25 minutes

We've got a whole section inspiring you to beanotto (see pages 42–5), but this one deserves its own page, due to the luxury of crunchy asparagus and the pistachio pesto. Adding spinach to the pesto makes it extra green, and mint and lemon are our little secret weapons to balance out the garlic and the saltiness of the Parmesan.

---

2 tbsp olive oil

1 onion / 3 spring onions, *finely chopped*

1 fat garlic clove, *roughly chopped*

150ml (5fl oz/¼ pint) white wine

570g (1lb 4½oz) jarred white beans, *with their bean stock*

120g (4¼oz) frozen peas

250g (9oz) asparagus, *woody ends trimmed*

salt and pepper

FOR THE PESTO

40g (1½oz) pine nuts

40g (1½oz) shelled pistachios, *chopped*

70g (2½oz) baby spinach leaves *(or use a mixed watercress, spinach and rocket salad bag)*

1 large garlic clove, *peeled*

10g (¼oz) basil

10g (¼oz) mint, *leaves roughly chopped*

zest and juice of ½ lemon, *plus wedges to serve*

50g (1¾oz) Parmesan or vegetarian hard cheese, *plus extra to serve*

3 tbsp extra virgin olive oil, *plus extra if needed*

1. Toast the pine nuts and pistachios for the pesto in a dry frying pan for about 3 minutes until lightly browned and aromatic, shaking the pan occasionally. Tip into a small bowl and set aside.

2. Put the pan back over a medium heat and add 1 tablespoon of the olive oil, followed by the onion or spring onions. Cook gently for about 8 minutes until softened (or just 3 minutes if using spring onions). Add the garlic and cook, stirring, for a further 2 minutes.

3. Meanwhile, make the pesto. Put 50g (1¾oz) of the toasted nuts, plus all the remaining pesto ingredients, into a food processor, and season. Blitz until you have a vibrant green paste; it should be fairly chunky, but add a splash more oil to loosen, if necessary. Check for seasoning and acidity, adding more lemon juice, if desired. Set aside.

4. Once the onion has softened, increase the heat slightly and pour in the wine. Allow to reduce for 2–3 minutes, then pour in the beans with their stock. Add a little water to the jar, give it a shake and pour that in too. Stir in the peas and reduce the heat to low. Simmer gently for 3–4 minutes, stirring gently, until the peas are defrosted and vivid green. Add more water to loosen, if desired.

5. Meanwhile, heat a griddle pan or frying pan over a medium heat. Add the asparagus, along with the remaining olive oil and a good pinch of sea salt, and fry for 3–4 minutes, tossing occasionally, until slightly charred.

6. Add the pesto to the bean pan. Season with plenty of cracked black pepper and stir to combine. Check for seasoning, adding more Parmesan, lemon juice or salt to taste.

7. Serve into bowls and top with the charred asparagus, extra Parmesan and the remaining toasted pine nuts and pistachios.

TOP TIP

If you've got extra greens lying around, add these with the onions – courgettes or fennel work really well!

PORCINI MUSHROOM BEANOTTO

Feeds 2
Takes 30 minutes

For this extra-special beanotto, we've put our own spin on a classic risotto combo: umami mushrooms, fragrant thyme, salty Parmesan and a crunchy pangrattato. The bean stock is crucial here, because it helps achieve that risotto-like texture. It's comforting, melt-in-your-mouth delicious, and is particularly good with a lemony salad on the side.

20g (¾oz) dried porcini mushrooms

200ml (7fl oz/⅓ pint) boiling water

300g (10½oz) mushrooms of your choice *(we like chestnut), sliced into bite-sized chunks*

25g (1oz) butter, *plus another knob to finish*

3 thyme or rosemary sprigs, *leaves picked*

1 onion, *roughly chopped*

2 garlic cloves, *thinly sliced*

150ml (5fl oz/¼ pint) white wine

570g (1lb 4½oz) jarred white beans, *with their bean stock*

15g (½oz) parsley, *leaves finely chopped*

25g (1oz) Parmesan or vegetarian hard cheese, *grated, plus extra to serve*

pepper

FOR THE PANGRATTATO

1 tbsp olive oil

50g (1¾oz) breadcrumbs

15g (½oz) parsley, *leaves very finely chopped*

1. Put the porcini mushrooms in a bowl and pour over the boiling water. Set aside to soak while you start your beanotto.

2. Dry-fry your mushrooms in a large frying pan over a medium–high heat, working in batches so you don't overcrowd the pan. Once they've browned and have lost most of their water (which will take about 5 minutes), transfer to a plate and repeat with the remaining batch(es). Once all the mushrooms have been fried, return them all to the pan, add the butter and reduce the heat to medium. Add the thyme or rosemary and the onion, and cook for 7–8 minutes, stirring often, until softened.

3. Add the garlic and cook for a further minute until fragrant, then increase the heat to high and pour in the wine. Cook for 4–5 minutes until there is virtually no liquid left in the mixture. At this point, add the porcini mushrooms, along with their soaking liquid, and cook for 2–3 minutes more until the liquid is reduced by half.

4. Reduce the heat to medium and stir through the beans and their bean stock. Keep cooking for about 10 minutes until the beanotto has reduced into a creamy consistency similar to that of a risotto. Add a splash of water or stock if it needs loosening.

5. While the beanotto is simmering away, make the pangrattato. Heat the olive oil in a separate frying pan over a medium heat, and stir in the breadcrumbs so they are coated in the oil. Fry for 4–5 minutes until crisp, making sure they don't burn. Remove from the heat, tip into a small bowl and stir through the chopped parsley.

6. The beanotto should look nice and creamy at this point. Just before serving, fold through a knob of butter and the Parmesan. Give the mixture a good grind of black pepper and serve in bowls. Finish with more Parmesan and the pangrattato.

> **TOP TIP**
> *If you are gluten-free or don't have any breadcrumbs, toasted pine nuts or pumpkin seeds mixed with sea salt and chopped fresh parsley is a banging alternative to the pangrattato.*

PERI PERI CHICKEN + LEMONY BEANS

Feeds 2–3
Takes 50 minutes, plus marinating

The Portuguese have their signature spicy chicken down to a tee when it comes to peri peri. This staple dish is bursting with bold, tangy flavours and makes for a hearty, comforting meal. This marinade is so packed with flavour, all you need is a bowl of lemony beans for a fresh and zesty side to balance out the heat.

4–6 bone-in, skin-on chicken thighs or a mixture of thighs and drumsticks

1 large red onion, *cut into 1cm (½in) wedges*

2 red peppers, *cored, deseeded and chopped into 3cm (1¼in) chunks*

salt and pepper

FOR THE WHITE BEAN BASE

2 tbsp olive oil

1 garlic clove, *crushed*

570g (1lb 4½oz) jarred white beans, *with their bean stock*

zest of ½ lemon, *plus wedges to serve*

100g (3½oz) leafy greens, such as spinach or kale *(optional)*

1 tbsp roughly chopped parsley

FOR THE MARINADE

2 tbsp olive oil

3 tbsp peri peri sauce, *plus extra to serve (shop-bought is fine)*

juice of 1 lemon

2 garlic cloves, peeled

1 tsp smoked paprika

1 tsp light soft brown sugar or honey

TO SERVE (OPTIONAL)

blanched Tenderstem broccoli or cavolo nero

buttered corn on the cob

Greek yoghurt or soured cream

1. Score the chicken skin (this allows the marinade to really soak in), then place the chicken pieces on a high-sided baking tray. Add the onion and red pepper chunks and season generously.

2. For ease, we're putting the marinade ingredients directly onto the chicken – so, drizzle the olive oil, peri peri sauce and lemon juice evenly all over the tray, then grate over the garlic and sprinkle over the smoked paprika and brown sugar or honey. Use your hands to spread the marinade thoroughly all over the chicken, then leave to marinate for 30 minutes, or overnight for a more intense flavour.

3. When you're ready to cook, preheat the oven to 200°C/180°C fan/400°F/gas mark 6.

4. Make sure all the chicken pieces are skin-side up, then roast for 40–45 minutes until the chicken is crispy and cooked through, and the peppers are nicely charred yet softened.

5. When the chicken and peppers have 10 minutes remaining, prepare the white bean base. Heat the olive oil in a saucepan over a medium heat. Add the garlic and cook for 1 minute until fragrant, then add the white beans and their bean stock, along with the lemon zest. If you have any greens that need using up, chuck these in, along with a splash of water. Cook for 3–4 minutes, stirring occasionally, until the beans are heated through and any greens are cooked. Check for seasoning, then stir in the fresh parsley.

6. Spread your bean base onto a serving plate. Remove the tray of peri peri chicken and peppers from the oven and pile them on top of the beans. Finish with a drizzle of juices from the roasting tray and a sprinkle of chopped parsley.

TOP TIP

For a veggie version, swap the chicken for 250g (9oz) halloumi, sliced into 5mm (¼in) slices, and reduce the roasting time to 15 minutes.

MUSHROOM RAGU + CHEESY BEAN BÉCHAMEL LASAGNE

Feeds 4–5
Takes 2 hours

There's something about those crispy edges and gooey middle bits that makes lasagne SO comforting. This veggie version has a classic sofrito base with woody herbs and mushrooms for both texture and umami. The secret ingredient? Beans, obviously — cooked down with butter, garlic, Parmesan and nutmeg, to make a velvety béchamel.

500g (1lb 2oz) chestnut mushrooms, *finely chopped*

5 tbsp olive oil

2 carrots, *finely diced*

1 celery stalk, *finely diced*

2 fresh or dried bay leaves

2 small onions, *finely chopped*

½ tsp sea salt

1 tbsp tomato purée

2 large garlic cloves, *crushed*

1 tsp dried mixed herbs or oregano

½ tsp dried chilli flakes

187ml (6½fl oz) red wine (1 mini bottle)

400g (14oz) can chopped tomatoes

150ml (5fl oz/¼ pint) veg stock

1 tsp caster sugar

14 dried lasagne sheets, *soaked for 10 minutes in warm water*

50g (1¾oz) mature Cheddar, *grated*

125g (4½oz) mozzarella, *drained*

pepper

FOR THE BEAN BÉCHAMEL

40g (1½oz) butter, *plus extra to grease and to dot on top*

2 garlic cloves, *diced*

570g (1lb 4½oz) jarred white beans, *with their bean stock*

1 tsp freshly grated nutmeg

100g (3½oz) Parmesan or vegetarian hard cheese, *grated, plus a little extra for between the layers*

1. Preheat the oven to 200°C/180°C fan/400°F/gas mark 6 and grease a 23 x 33cm (9 x 13in) baking dish with butter.

2. Dry-fry the mushrooms in a large, deep pan over a medium heat for 6–7 minutes until softened – you may need to do this in batches. Remove from the pan and set aside.

3. In the same pan, heat the olive oil and add the carrots, celery, bay leaves and onions, along with the salt. It may seem like a lot of oil but, without meat, you need to bring in the fat from somewhere. Stir well to coat the veggies, then sweat for 15–20 minutes, stirring occasionally, until the ingredients are beginning to soften and have shrunk significantly.

4. Add the tomato purée, garlic, herbs and chilli flakes, and cook for a further minute, then return the mushrooms to the pan. Stir and cook for another minute. If there is still some liquid in the pan from the mushrooms, cook for a little longer until this is reduced and some of the base begins to stick to the bottom of the pan.

5. Pour in the red wine, deglazing any veg that has begun to caramelise at the bottom. Allow the alcohol to cook off for 5–8 minutes.

6. Tip in the chopped tomatoes, then fill the can about a third full of water, give it a swirl and throw that in too. Add the veg stock, followed by a pinch of salt and the sugar, and bubble for 15 minutes.

7. Meanwhile, for the bean béchamel, melt the butter in a saucepan over a low heat. Add the garlic and cook for 1 minute before adding the beans and their bean stock. Fill the jar about a third full of water, give it a swirl, and throw that in too, along with the nutmeg and Parmesan. Bring to a simmer for 1 minute. Use a wooden spoon to break up most of the beans, leaving a few whole for texture. Check for seasoning, then remove from the heat.

8. Spoon a few ladles of the mushroom ragu sauce into the bottom of the prepared baking dish, and top with a single layer of the pre-soaked lasagne sheets. Add another layer of mushroom ragu, followed by a few spoonfuls of bean béchamel. Tear over a third of the mozzarella, then top with black pepper and some grated Parmesan.

9. Repeat this process twice more, finishing the final layer by scattering over all the Cheddar and the remaining mozzarella. Dot with a few more knobs of butter for an extra golden finish, if you like. Bake for 35 minutes, or until golden on top.

10. Serve the lasagne in the centre of the table for guests to help themselves. It's particularly delicious with a petit pois and rocket salad, dressed with olive oil, lemon juice, Dijon mustard and shavings of Parmesan – we're just saying…

CHERRY TOMATO, ANCHOVY + WHITE BEAN GRATIN

Feeds 4–6
Takes 45 minutes

Sweet cherry tomatoes and salty anchovies make up the base of this wow-worthy gratin. We've swapped cream for lighter crème fraîche and suggest pairing it with a zingy chicory and caper salad to balance out all the flavours. It's also delicious with charred lemony broccoli if you prefer to keep it simple.

- 50g (1¾oz) canned anchovies in olive oil
- 3 fat garlic cloves, halved
- 1 rosemary sprig, leaves picked and finely chopped
- ½ teaspoon dried chilli flakes (optional)
- 600g (1lb 5oz) cherry plum tomatoes
- 30g (1oz) basil, leaves picked and stalks finely chopped
- splash of red wine vinegar
- 1 tsp white or brown sugar (optional)
- 2 × 570g (1lb 4½oz) jars white beans, with their bean stock
- 4 heaped tbsp crème fraîche
- zest of 1 lemon
- 50g (1¾oz) Parmesan or pecorino or vegetarian hard cheese, grated
- 50g (1¾oz) Gruyère or Cheddar
- 100g (3½oz) breadcrumbs
- 2 tbsp olive oil
- salt and pepper

FOR THE CHICORY SALAD
- 4 chicory bulbs
- 2 tbsp sherry vinegar
- 2 tbsp capers, drained
- 4 tbsp extra virgin olive oil

1. Tip the anchovies and their olive oil into a medium saucepan over a medium heat. Add the garlic, rosemary and chilli flakes, if using, and cook for 1 minute until the anchovies start to sizzle and melt.

2. Tumble in the cherry plum tomatoes and basil. Cover the pan with a lid and give it a vigorous shake to coat the tomatoes in the oil. Reduce the heat to low and simmer for 25–30 minutes, or until the tomatoes have softened and broken down. Stir halfway through, adding the vinegar and sugar to taste, if using.

3. Add the white beans with their bean stock, and stir to combine into the tomatoey juices. Then add the crème fraîche and lemon zest, and season to taste with salt and plenty of cracked black pepper. Increase the heat to medium and let the beans bubble for 5–6 minutes until you have a slightly thickened, creamy stew.

4. Meanwhile, in a small bowl, mix together the Parmesan or pecorino, Gruyère or Cheddar, breadcrumbs, some cracked black pepper and the olive oil.

5. Preheat the grill to medium. Decant the contents of the saucepan into an ovenproof dish. Sprinkle the cheesy breadcrumbs over the top, then pop under the grill for 3–4 minutes, or until golden, checking often so it doesn't burn.

6. Meanwhile, make the salad. Discard the woody ends of the chicory bulbs, then separate the leaves and slice them thinly. Put into a bowl with the rest of the ingredients and toss well to coat.

7. Leave the gratin to sit for a few minutes before serving with the salad.

TOP TIP
This recipe is great for a dinner party if you're the kind of host who wants to make everything ahead of time and swan around with a glass of wine in hand...

MEXICAN-INSPIRED BEAN SALAD WITH CRISPY TORTILLA CROUTONS

Feeds 3–4
Takes 15 minutes

(V)

MÓNICA ALAZRAKI

While Mónica Alazraki's version of Mexican *ensalada de nopales* doesn't include *nopal* (prickly pear cactus), it still echoes the salad's fresh flavours of coriander, jalapeño and lime. 'My mum used to make it very often for lunch; it's based on a traditional salad that is a national staple in Mexican cuisine. It's both delicious and nutritious.'

---

2 large, soft corn tortillas, cut into strips

1 tbsp neutral oil, such as sunflower or rapeseed oil

3 tomatoes, finely chopped

1 small onion, diced into small cubes

1 avocado, diced into small cubes

570g (1lb 4½oz) jarred white beans, drained and rinsed

1 tsp dried oregano

100g (3½oz) feta, cut into small cubes

4 tbsp extra virgin olive oil

juice of 2 limes

30g (1oz) coriander, finely chopped

1 jalapeño chilli, finely chopped (optional)

salt and pepper

1. Preheat your oven to 200°C/180°C fan/400°F/gas mark 6 and line a baking tray with baking paper.

2. Arrange the strips of tortilla on the prepared tray. Drizzle with the oil, season with a pinch of flaky sea salt, and bake for 4–6 minutes until deeply golden and crisp. Remove from the oven and allow to cool.

3. In a large mixing bowl, gently combine the tomatoes, onion, avocado, white beans and oregano. Add the feta, extra virgin olive oil and lime juice, and stir to combine. Test for seasoning and adjust if necessary. Finish with the chopped coriander and jalapeño, if using.

4. Scoop into 3–4 bowls and sprinkle over the crispy tortilla strips to serve.

BAKED BEANS

If you're a long-standing member of the Bold Bean community, you'll be well aware that we have a range of much-loved baked beans.

We lovingly made these to fill a gap for adults who've 'grown-out' of the classic tin of baked beans, as well as people who think they hate baked beans, and, crucially, bean lovers who are short on time but want something satisfying and DELICIOUS. Many serve them up on buttered toast with gratings of Cheddar, but what we didn't anticipate was how many of you wanted to use them as ingredients in their own right, speeding up suppers that have all the flavour of hours spent on the stove. So, here you go: a few ideas, recipes and hacks with our baked beans range.

CLASSIC BAKED BEANS

Our tangiest variety of baked beans has a hit of nostalgia that lends itself well to fattier flavours, such as bacon or crispy fried eggs.

SWAP IDEAS
Sub out the red beans and serve Classic Baked Beans alongside our Cheesy Bean Brunch Hotcakes on page 121. Or skip steps 2 and 3 in the Sausage + Butter Bean Stew on page 27, instead using 2 jars of Classic Baked Beans.

PASTA ALLA GUANCIALE

150g (5½oz) dried pasta

1 tbsp olive oil

100g (3½oz) guanciale or pancetta, cut into small strips

1–2 garlic cloves, finely chopped

½ tsp dried chilli flakes (optional)

325g (11½oz) jar Classic Baked Beans

30g (1oz) Parmesan or vegetarian hard cheese, grated, plus extra to serve

handful of parsley, chopped

rocket salad, to serve

1. Cook the pasta in salted boiling water according to the packet instructions until al dente, then drain, reserving a cup of the pasta water.

2. Meanwhile, heat the olive oil in a large frying pan over a medium heat. Add the guanciale or pancetta and cook for 4–5 minutes until crisp and golden and the fat has rendered.

3. Remove the guanciale from the pan with a slotted spoon. Pour off most of the fat, leaving about 1 tablespoon in the pan. Stir in the garlic and the dried chilli flakes, if using. Cook for 1 minute until fragrant. Add the baked beans, stirring to coat in the guanciale fat and garlic, and warm through.

4. Combine the cooked pasta, crispy guanciale and beans, tossing to coat. Add a splash of the reserved pasta water to create a glossy sauce. Stir in the Parmesan and parsley. Season with pepper and serve immediately, with extra Parmesan and a rocket salad.

BAKED BEANS continued

RICH TOMATO BAKED BEANS

We created these after being inspired by how the Greeks cook their *gigantes plaki*. Herby, rich and warming, they make the perfect partners for pasta, a wonderful sauce for aubergine parmigiana or a delightful accompaniment to simple grilled fish.

MED-VEG, BLACK OLIVE + FETA BAKE

2 tbsp olive oil

1 red onion, thinly sliced

1 pepper, cored, deseeded and diced

3 garlic cloves, finely chopped

2 × 325g (11½oz) jars Rich Tomato Baked Beans

pinch of dried chilli flakes (optional)

50g (1¾oz) black olives

1 tbsp capers, rinsed

200g (7oz) feta

pinch of dried oregano

1. Preheat your oven to 180°C/160°C fan/350°F/gas mark 4. Heat the olive oil in a large, ovenproof frying pan over a medium–high heat. Add the onion and pepper, season, and cook for 7–8 minutes until softened and starting to caramelise. Add the garlic and cook for 1 more minute.

2. Stir through the beans and dried chilli flakes, if you like a bit of heat. Fill the empty jar about a third full with water, shake, then add that too. Stir through the olives and capers. Nestle the block of feta in the centre of the pan, with a pinch of dried oregano on top.

3. Transfer the pan to the oven and bake for 10–12 minutes, or until the feta is just golden at the edges and slightly oozy in the middle. Finish with a sprinkle of freshly chopped parsley, if you like, and some lemon zest. Serve hot – we like to add crusty bread for dipping.

SMOKY CHILLI BAKED BEANS

We had to do a chilli take on the baked bean, with smoky chipotle running through a rich tomato-and-bean sauce. For the chilli-heads, we upped the ante a bit with some chilli flakes. Of course, the obvious move is to serve these beans in Mexican dishes – in tacos, as a chilli, or in cheesy quesadillas – but we also love making them into a shakshuka of sorts, with pickled red onions and Greek yoghurt.

CHEESY BEAN QUESADILLAS

1 tbsp neutral oil, *such as sunflower or rapeseed oil*

2 large tortillas

325g (11½oz) jar Smoky Chilli Baked Beans

50g (1¾ oz) Cheddar, *grated*

sliced avocado

pickled red onions

soured cream

a handful of coriander, *chopped*

lime wedges

1. Heat the oil in a non-stick frying pan over a medium heat. Add a large tortilla to the pan and pour half of the beans onto one side. Gently mash some of the beans for a creamier texture.

2. Sprinkle with half the cheese and fold the tortilla over. Press down with a spatula and cook for 2–3 minutes until the cheese starts to melt, then carefully flip the quesadilla over to get an even golden colour.

3. Repeat this with the other tortilla and the remaining beans and cheese. Slice the quesadillas into wedges and serve with sliced avocado, pickled red onions, a dollop of soured cream, coriander and lime wedges on the side for squeezing over.

AWARD-WINNING FARMER

" IMAGINE THE EXCITEMENT OF A NEW TECHNOLOGY THAT NEEDED ONLY SUNSHINE, RAIN AND SOIL TO CREATE NITROGEN FERTILISER OUT OF THIN AIR; ITS BY-PRODUCTS, THE MOST SUSTAINABLE OF HUMAN PROTEINS AND FOOD FOR POLLINATING INSECTS. WELL, THE GOOD NEWS IS THAT THIS TECHNOLOGY EXISTS – THE BEAN PLANT...FIVE THOUSAND YEARS AGO, EGYPTIANS BURIED THEIR DEAD WITH BEANS TO ASSIST IN A TRANSITION TO THE AFTERLIFE. TODAY, BEANS HAVE A KEY ROLE TO PLAY IN A REAL-WORLD TRANSITION. A REGENERATIVE FOOD SUPPLY NEEDS BEANS AS AN INTEGRAL PART OF OUR FARMING SYSTEMS. "

– *Andy Cato*

BLACK BEANS

Small, dark and earthy, black beans are great at balancing fresh, crunchy ingredients. And when simmered, they become truly velvety.

SWEETCORN + BLACK BEAN FRITTERS WITH TOMATO + RED ONION SALSA

Feeds 2–3
Takes 45 minutes

Eggs on toast are great, but have you ever tasted eggs on black bean fritters? We HIGHLY recommend these for a brunch twist. The starchiness from the beans means they hold their shape really well, and there's a subtle sweetness (and added texture) from the sweetcorn. Any leftovers are delicious cold, with cream cheese and tomato chutney.

198g (7oz) can sweetcorn, drained, liquid reserved

½ large red onion / 2 spring onions, finely chopped

½ × 570g (1lb 4½oz) jarred black beans, drained and rinsed

3 tbsp plain flour

2 tsp smoked paprika

2 tsp ground cumin

1 egg, beaten

100ml (3½fl oz) light olive oil or neutral oil, such as sunflower or rapeseed oil, for shallow-frying

salt and pepper

FOR THE SALSA

½ large red onion / 2 spring onions, finely chopped

100g (3½oz) cherry tomatoes, finely chopped

½ × 570g (1lb 4½oz) jar black beans, drained and rinsed

zest and juice of 1 lime

handful of coriander, finely chopped, plus extra to serve

1 red bird's-eye or normal red chilli, deseeded and roughly chopped

pinch of white or brown sugar (optional)

TO SERVE

a dollop of natural yoghurt

hot sauce or sriracha, for drizzling

2–3 fried or poached eggs

sliced avocado (optional)

1. Start by making the salsa. Combine all the ingredients in a bowl and mix well, then season with a pinch of salt. Taste and add a pinch of sugar if your tomatoes aren't very sweet/ripe. Put the salsa to one side.

2. For the fritters, tip the sweetcorn, red onion and black beans into a large bowl, followed by the flour, smoked paprika and cumin. Season, then add 1 tablespoon of the reserved juice from the sweetcorn can, along with the beaten egg, and mix well to combine. Some of the beans will mush into the batter, helping to hold the mixture together when they're fried.

3. Heat the oil in a medium frying pan over a medium heat, ensuring the bottom is completely coated with enough oil to try the fritters. Working in batches, scoop 2 heaped tablespoons of the batter for each fritter and add to the pan, spreading it out a little with the back of the spoon. You want them to be about 2cm (¾in) in height, so still quite chunky. Add as many as you can fit in the pan without overcrowding. Cook for 4–5 minutes on each side until golden and crispy. Remove from the pan with a slotted spoon and set aside on a plate lined with paper towels while you fry the rest. This mixture should make about 8 fritters.

4. Divide the fritters between plates. Top each stack of fritters with a dollop of yoghurt, a few coriander leaves, a drizzle of hot sauce or sriracha, a fried or poached egg, and maybe some sliced avocado, if you like. Serve the salsa on the side to prevent it from making the fritters go soggy.

TOP TIP

To make this dairy-free, simply omit the natural yoghurt on top. For gluten-free, use cornflour in the fritters instead of plain flour.

COLD SESAME BLACK BEAN NOODLES

Feeds 2
Takes 10–15 minutes

(V) (Ve) (D)

SUSANNA BOWERS

This recipe has all the flavours of Sichuan dan-dan noodles, but Susanna Bowers adds black beans for an extra protein hit. In her delicious recipe, creamy tahini is whisked into a sauce, along with sweet maple syrup, fiery ginger, spicy chilli oil and soy sauce. It's so quick to make – you can whip up the sauce in the time it takes for the noodles to cook!

180g (6¼oz) soba, rice or wheat noodles

100g (3½oz) greens, such as Tenderstem broccoli, green beans or kale

1½ tbsp tahini

2 tbsp soy sauce

1 tsp chilli oil, plus extra to serve

juice of ½ lime, plus wedges to serve

thumb-sized piece of fresh ginger, finely grated

1 small garlic clove, finely grated

1 tsp maple syrup

about 3 tbsp warm water

½ × 570g (1lb 4½oz) jar black beans, drained and rinsed

1 tbsp sesame oil

50g (1¾oz) edamame beans (optional)

salt

TO SERVE

½ cucumber, peeled, halved lengthways, deseeded and chopped

2 spring onions, finely sliced

coriander leaves

sesame seeds

crispy onions (optional)

chopped roasted peanuts (optional)

1. Bring a pan of salted water to the boil and cook the noodles according to the packet instructions. Cook your greens of choice at the same time in the same pan until tender.

2. Meanwhile, in a large serving bowl, mix together the tahini, soy sauce, chilli oil, lime juice, ginger, garlic and maple syrup. Add the warm water a tablespoon at a time until you reach a smooth consistency, similar to that of natural yoghurt.

3. Tip the black beans into the sauce and mix well to coat.

4. Once cooked, drain the veg and noodles and rinse with cold water. Drizzle with the sesame oil to prevent sticking, then tip them into the sauce, along with the edamame beans, if using, and toss to coat.

5. Divide the noodles between bowls and top with the cucumber chunks, spring onions, coriander, a sprinkling of sesame seeds, a drizzle of chilli oil for some extra heat and crispy onions or chopped roasted peanuts for some crunch, if you like. Finish with a squeeze of lime.

PUNCHY PEANUT, GINGER + BLACK BEAN CURRY WITH BUTTERED WILD RICE

Feeds 2
Takes 10–15 minutes

This curry is a flavour powerhouse that packs a punch thanks to plenty of fiery fresh ginger and those small-but-mighty bird's-eye chillies. There's a little hint of sweetness from the red onion and the peppers, earthy umami from the mushrooms and creamy nuttiness from the peanut butter, and the black beans add their own delicious flavour.

200g (7oz) red, black or wild rice *(optional)*

2 tbsp neutral oil, *such as sunflower or rapeseed oil*

1 red onion, *sliced*

2 red or orange peppers, *cored, deseeded and sliced into 2–3cm (¾–1¼ in) strips*

150g (5½oz) closed-cup mushrooms, *sliced*

large thumb-sized piece of fresh ginger, *peeled and thinly sliced*

1 tbsp medium curry powder

1 tbsp tomato purée

2 tbsp peanut butter *(crunchy or smooth – try a deep-roasted one for more flavour)*

½–1 red bird's-eye chilli, *deseeded and finely sliced*

50ml (2fl oz) water

15 fresh curry leaves, *roughly torn (optional)*

400g (14oz) can chopped tomatoes

570g (1lb 4½oz) jarred black beans, *with bean stock*

hot sauce, *to taste (optional)*

few handfuls of spinach, kale or salad leaves

knob of salted butter *(optional)*

salt

TO SERVE

small handful of coriander leaves

1 lime, *quartered*

dried chilli flakes *(optional)*

1. If serving with rice, start by cooking it according to the packet instructions (it can sit there with the lid on, staying warm, if it's done early).

2. For the curry, heat the oil in a medium saucepan over a medium heat. Tip in the onion and peppers, along with a pinch of salt, and cook for around 10 minutes, stirring occasionally, until soft.

3. Add the mushrooms and ginger, along with another small pinch of salt, and fry for a further 5–6 minutes until the mushrooms have softened and the ginger is smelling delish.

4. Add the curry powder, tomato purée, peanut butter and chilli, along with the measured water to loosen. Stir in the curry leaves, if using, and mix to create a paste. Continue to cook for 2–3 minutes, stirring frequently so that the peanut butter doesn't catch on the bottom of the pan.

5. Pour in the chopped tomatoes, then fill the can about a third full of water, give it a swirl, and throw that in too. Add the black beans and their bean stock, and stir. Simmer, still over a medium heat, for 15 minutes until the curry has slightly reduced and is looking glossy and thick. If it's looking too thick, add a little more water. Check the seasoning, adding a bit of hot sauce if you want more punch! Add a few handfuls of any spinach, kale or salad leaves you have – a perfect way to use up any sad lettuce bags in the refrigerator – and stir these through for a bit of greenery.

6. When you're ready to serve, take the lid off the rice, if using, and stir through the salted butter – this is optional, but it will give the rice a glossier, more buttery texture and taste. Spoon the rice into bowls and top with the curry. Serve with a generous sprinkle of coriander leaves, lime wedges for squeezing and a scattering of chilli flakes, if you like.

TOP TIP
The curry leaves are not essential, but if you can find them, they will definitely amp up the flavour!

BLACK BEAN MAKHANI WITH KACHUMBER SALAD

Feeds 4
Takes 30 minutes

 RAINA PATEL

A makhani (originally a Punjabi word for butter) simply OOZES comfort. Here, Bold Bean contributor Raina Patel replaces lentils with black beans to create a delicious veggie makhani that's packed with flavour. She says: 'This recipe is my tribute to my grandma – cosy, comforting flavours from my childhood with a little twist.'

2 tbsp neutral oil, such as sunflower or rapeseed oil

1 onion, roughly chopped

3 garlic cloves, crushed or finely grated

thumb-sized piece of fresh ginger, finely grated

1 chilli, finely chopped / ½ tsp cayenne pepper, to taste

3 tsp garam masala

1 tsp ground cumin

1 tsp paprika

1 tsp ground turmeric

150ml (5fl oz/¼ pint) passata / 2 large tomatoes, blitzed in a blender

1 bay leaf (optional)

570g (1lb 4½oz) jarred black beans, with their bean stock

100ml (3½fl oz) double cream or Greek yoghurt

pinch of white sugar (optional)

juice of 2 limes, plus wedges to serve

salt

Greek or coconut yoghurt, to serve

FOR THE KACHUMBER SALAD

½ cucumber, diced

2 vine or cherry tomatoes, diced

½ red onion, very finely chopped

2 tbsp lemon juice

pinch of chilli powder

small handful of mint or coriander

1. Heat the oil in a large saucepan over a medium heat. Tip in the onion with a pinch of salt, and cook for 8–10 minutes until softened. Add the garlic, ginger and chilli or cayenne pepper, and cook for a further 2–3 minutes until fragrant.

2. Stir in the garam masala, cumin, paprika, turmeric and another good pinch of salt. Continue to cook for 1 minute or so, stirring constantly to prevent the spices from burning. Add a splash of water if it begins to stick.

3. Add the passata and the bay leaf, if using, and stir for 2–3 minutes. The mixture will begin to thicken. Now add the beans and their bean stock. Increase the heat to medium–high and bring the mixture to a gentle boil. Once bubbling, reduce the heat to a simmer and cook for about 10 minutes, stirring occasionally to prevent sticking. Add a splash of water if needed.

4. Meanwhile, make the kachumber salad. Combine all the ingredients in a bowl and taste for seasoning. Set aside for later.

5. If you're happy with a chunkier makhani, you could partially mash the beans with a potato masher, then add the cream or yoghurt. However, for something closer to the traditional Punjabi classic, carefully transfer a third of the mixture to a blender, making sure the bay leaf isn't in there. Pour in a splash of the cream or yoghurt to cool it slightly, secure the lid tightly, and blend until smooth. Pour the blended mixture back into the pot and stir to combine.

6. Taste for seasoning. At this stage, you may want to add a little sugar to balance. Stir in the remaining cream or yoghurt. Add the lime a little at a time, tasting as you go.

7. To serve, spoon the makhani into bowls, and top each one with a dollop of Greek or coconut yoghurt and a big spoonful of the kachumber salad. To make into a full and hearty meal, serve with basmati rice, naans or tortilla chips.

BEEF + BLACK BEAN PICADILLO BAKE WITH SWEET POTATOES AND CREOLE SALSA

Feeds 2
Takes 10–15 minutes

STEPHEN BLADES

Picar is Spanish, meaning 'to mince', so think of this dish as a kind of Latin American minced-meat hash. Picadillos vary depending on where you are in the world, but Stephen Blades's version takes its cues from Cuba's sweet-and-sour flavour combos, folding our black beans into the mix.

---

1 tbsp neutral oil, *such as sunflower or rapeseed oil*
1 large onion, *finely chopped*
2 peppers (any colour), *cored, deseeded and finely chopped*
1 red or green jalapeño chilli, *finely chopped (optional)*
4 garlic cloves, *grated*
250g (9oz) minced beef
2 tbsp tomato purée
2 tsp ground coriander
2 tsp ground cumin
2 tsp dried oregano
2 tsp smoked paprika
400g (14oz) can chopped tomatoes
570g (1lb 4½oz) jarred black beans, *with their bean stock*
75g (2¾oz) green olives, *halved*
1 beef stock cube, *crumbled*
75g (2¾oz) raisins
2 tbsp capers
2 tbsp red wine vinegar or white wine vinegar
1 tsp light soft brown sugar
20g (¾oz) coriander, *chopped*
100g (3½oz) Cheddar, *grated*
salt and pepper

FOR THE ROASTED SWEET POTATOES
750g (1lb 10oz) whole sweet potatoes, *skins left on*
1 tbsp olive oil

1. Preheat the oven to 200°C/180°C fan/400°F/gas mark 6 and place a sheet of foil on the middle shelf.

2. Rub the sweet potatoes all over with the olive oil and some salt. Pierce the skins several times with a sharp knife and place directly on the top shelf of the oven (the foil below will catch any syrup). Bake for 1 hour.

3. Meanwhile, get your picadillo ready. Heat the oil in a large ovenproof frying pan over a medium heat. Add the onion and peppers, along with a pinch of salt, and cook for 8–10 minutes until soft. Add the chilli, if using, and the garlic, and fry for a further 2 minutes.

4. Increase the heat slightly, then add the minced beef, breaking it up with the back of your spoon. Fry for 5–8 minutes until browned. Stir in the tomato purée and all the spices, along with a good pinch of salt and a small splash of water, and cook for a further 2–3 minutes, until the purée deepens in colour.

5. Add all the remaining ingredients, except the coriander and cheese. Bring to a simmer. Half-fill the empty bean jar with water and add that too. Cook for about 30 minutes until all the flavours have combined, the beef is tender and the mixture is thick. You may want to stir it a few times to check it's not catching on the bottom.

6. Meanwhile, prepare the salsa by combining all the ingredients in a small bowl. Season to taste.

7. Once the picadillo looks ready, taste and add salt and pepper if needed, then stir through most of the coriander, saving some for a garnish.

8. Check if the potatoes are done by piercing with a cutlery knife; if there is no resistance, remove them from the oven and cover to keep warm.

9. Once your potatoes are done, preheat the grill to medium. Sprinkle the grated Cheddar over the picadillo and grill until melted and golden. Top with most of the remaining coriander leaves.

10. Move the potatoes to a serving platter and split open their skins to reveal the soft orange flesh. Spoon over the salsa and scatter over a few more coriander leaves. Serve with the picadillo.

FOR THE CREOLE SALSA

3 cherry or plum tomatoes, *finely chopped*

½ red onion, *finely chopped*

1–2 red or green jalapeño chillies, *finely chopped*

10g (¼oz) parsley, *chopped*

10g (¼oz) coriander, *chopped*

1 tsp hot sauce

juice of 2 limes

1 tbsp olive oil

TOP TIP

Use whichever hot sauce you like for the salsa – we love Tabasco, sriracha or Cholula.

SPICY BEAN PARATHA POCKETS

Feeds 3
Takes 30 minutes

SHEEL PATEL

This cheesy, gently-spiced dish is brilliant when you want something quick and healthy. 'Frozen parathas and hearty beans are my go-to for busy days,' Bold Bean contributor Sheel Patel says, 'creating a protein-packed, pizza-like dish with minimal prep. It's a simple, one-pan meal perfect for weeknights, paired with a fresh salad and minty raita.'

---

2 tbsp olive oil

1 tsp cumin seeds

1 small onion, *finely chopped*

3 garlic cloves, *finely minced*

1 green or red chilli, *deseeded and finely chopped (optional)*

1 tsp chilli powder

½ tsp ground turmeric

1 tsp ground coriander

1 large tomato, *finely chopped*

½ × 570g (1lb 4½oz) jar black beans, *drained*

6 frozen parathas *(available in most supermarkets)*

150g (5½oz) mozzarella and/or Cheddar, *grated*

2 tbsp oil or melted butter, *for frying the parathas*

FOR THE MINT RAITA

large handful of mint leaves, *chopped*

150g (5½oz) Greek yoghurt

small pinch of ground cumin

zest and juice of 1 lemon

1 small garlic clove, *grated*

pinch sea salt

TO SERVE

green salad

mango chutney

1. Heat the olive oil in a pan over a medium heat. Once hot, add the cumin seeds and wait until you hear them sizzle. Cook for a minute or so, then add the onion, along with a pinch of salt, and cook for 8–10 minutes until soft and translucent.

2. Meanwhile, combine all the raita ingredients in a small bowl and taste for seasoning. Adjust to your preference.

3. Back to the onion pan. Add the garlic, the chilli, if using, and ground spices. Fry for a few minutes until fragrant, then stir in the tomato and the black beans. Cook for about 5 minutes until the flavours combine, then use a potato masher or fork to crush the beans lightly, leaving some chunky for texture.

4. Take your first frozen paratha and heat in a dry frying pan over a medium-high heat for no more than 30 seconds. This will help the paratha become more flexible. Then take 2–3 heaped tablespoons of the bean mixture and place in the centre of the paratha. Add some grated cheese, then fold over the paratha. If you like, you can use a fork to bind the edges or, if your paratha is looking a little full, just fold it over and let the cheese melt to stick it together. Set aside and repeat with the remaining parathas and filling.

5. Brush the parathas with a little oil or butter, and fry for about 4 minutes on each side until golden brown – you may need to do this in batches depending on the size of your pan. Let them cool a little, then dig in! Enjoy with a fresh green salad and a scoop of raita, along with some mango chutney for sweetness!

TOP TIP

The filling can be made the day before and stored in an airtight container in the refrigerator until needed.

BLACK BEAN, BEETROOT + WALNUT DIP

Feeds 6
Takes 10 minutes, plus soaking time

 JANE HART

This dip is the perfect balance of sweet and sour, thanks to a dash of maple syrup and lots of lemon juice, a flavour pairing that goes seriously well with the earthy beetroot and walnuts. Bold Bean contributor Jane Hart dreamed up this recipe: 'It's versatile, delicious, and pairs beautifully with roasted summer veggies or with crumbled blue Stilton in winter.

12 walnut halves
250g (9oz) vacuum-packed cooked beetroot, drained
2 tsp maple syrup
juice of 2 lemons
570g (1lb 4½oz) jarred black beans, with their bean stock
1 tsp cumin seeds
50g (1¾oz) pumpkin or sunflower seeds
salt

TO SERVE
toasted pittas
vegetable crudités

1. If you have time, soak the walnuts in cold water for 30 minutes, then drain. This step is optional, but it prevents that astringent walnut flavour!

2. Put the walnuts, beetroots and maple syrup into a food processor with the juice of 1 lemon and whizz to a smooth paste. (If using a small blender, at this point tip the whizzed beetroot into a large bowl before adding the black beans to the blender, then combine.)

3. Add the black beans to the blender, along with their bean stock, and whizz again. Taste for seasoning and add a little salt and more lemon juice if needed.

4. Toast the cumin seeds and pumpkin or sunflower seeds in a dry frying pan over a medium–high heat for 2–3 minutes. Once they start to pop and smell toasty, remove from the heat and let them cool slightly.

5. Spoon the dip into a bowl and top with the toasted seeds. Serve with your chosen accompaniments – we like either piping hot fluffy pittas or colourful, crunchy crudités.

TOP TIP
Add chicken or veg stock to any leftover dip and turn it into a wholesome soup, best enjoyed with a hunk of crusty bread.

BLACK BEAN-STUFFED PEPPER FEAST WITH YOGHURT + A POMEGRANATE SALAD

Feeds 6
Takes 1 hour

This is a feast that will really get your guests oohing and aahing. It does require a little more effort, but for a special occasion and special company, it's ABSOLUTELY worth it. The spiced filling works a dream alongside the cooling yoghurt dip, with the sweet pomegranate salad adding aromatics and freshness to bring this whole feast together.

---

6 large peppers (red, orange or yellow), halved, cored and deseeded

3 tbsp olive oil

1 red onion, finely chopped

2 tbsp tomato purée

1½ tsp ground allspice

1 tsp sumac

2 tsp dried mint

1 tsp ground cumin

1 tsp dried cinnamon

4 garlic cloves, roughly chopped

2 × 570g (1lb 4½oz) jarred black beans, drained

salt and pepper

40g (1½oz) pistachios, to garnish (optional)

FOR THE YOGHURT DIP

450g (1lb) strained yoghurt

juice of 1 lemon

pinch of flaky sea salt

FOR THE POMEGRANATE SALAD

1 red onion, halved and thinly sliced into half-moons

1 cucumber, deseeded and roughly sliced

2 tsp sumac

200g (7oz) pomegranate seeds

15–30g (½–1oz) fresh mint and/or dill, leaves roughly chopped

juice of 1 lemon

olive oil, for drizzling

pomegranate molasses, for drizzling (optional)

1. To make the yoghurt dip, mix together the yoghurt and lemon juice in a bowl and season with salt. Refrigerate until needed.

2. Preheat the oven to 200°C/180°C fan/400°F/gas mark 6. Line a large baking tray with baking paper.

3. Place the pepper halves, cut side up, on the prepared tray. Brush with ½ tablespoon of the oil, season, then roast for 20 minutes until just tender and slightly charred in places.

4. Meanwhile, heat 2 tablespoons of the olive oil in a large pan over a medium heat. Add the onion, along with a pinch of salt, and cook for 8–10 minutes, stirring regularly, until softened. Add the tomato purée, all of the dried herbs and spices and the garlic, and cook for a further 3 minutes until fragrant. Add a splash of water to loosen, if necessary.

5. Tip the drained black beans into the pan and stir through until fully coated in the spices. Lightly mash a few of the beans with the back of a fork or a spatula – this will help to thicken and provide more moisture to the mixture. Let the bean mix bubble away for 6–7 minutes.

6. When the peppers have cooled a bit, lightly tear them to open them up a bit more. Roughly divide the bean mixture into 6 portions and, with a spoon, use each portion to fill 2 pepper halves. Brush with the remaining oil and roast for 10–15 minutes, until the filling is piping hot and the outsides look soft.

7. Meanwhile, if you're garnishing the dish with pistachios, cook these in a dry frying pan for about 5 minutes, or until golden and smelling toasty. Roughly chop and set aside.

8. You can also start on the salad. In a bowl, combine all the ingredients with a pinch of salt and mix well. Finish with a drizzle of olive oil.

9. When you're ready to serve, use the back of a spoon to spread the yoghurt dip across the base of a large serving platter. Lay the stuffed peppers evenly on top and scatter over the chopped pistachios, if using. Serve alongside the pomegranate salad, drizzled with a little pomegranate molasses (if you like) – you could serve this with warm flatbreads too.

SEEDED CAPER, SHALLOT + PARMESAN BLACK BEAN SALAD

Feeds 2, or 4 as a side
Takes 15 minutes

The secret to a good salad is getting every element in each bite. Here, small but nutty black beans get friendly with radishes, plump raisins and toasted sunflower seeds, with generous gratings of Parmesan for an umami hit. The fresh, herby, sharp caper vinaigrette brings it all together. It's an unusual combo, delicious with roasted chicken legs.

70g (2½oz) sunflower seeds

90g (3¼oz) rocket

8 radishes, *thinly sliced*

570g (1lb 4½oz) jarred black beans, *drained and rinsed*

75g (2¾oz) Parmesan or vegetarian hard cheese

salt and pepper

FOR THE CAPER VINAIGRETTE

1–2 tbsp baby capers *(or big ones), roughly chopped*

50g (1¾oz) jumbo raisins or sultanas

1 tbsp white wine vinegar or red wine vinegar

2 tbsp extra virgin olive oil

1 tsp Dijon mustard

1 small shallot, *finely chopped*

30g (1oz) chives and/or parsley, *finely chopped*

1. In a small bowl, whisk together all the ingredients for the vinaigrette until well combined – do this first to let the shallots mellow and the raisins plump up. Season to taste.

2. Toast the sunflower seeds in a dry frying pan over a medium–high heat for 3–4 minutes until they start to turn golden and smell toasty.

3. Tip the rocket, radishes, seeds and black beans into a large mixing bowl. Coarsely grate in about half of the Parmesan – coarsely grating will give you bigger pieces with a bit more bite, which we really love. Drizzle half of the herbed vinaigrette over the salad and toss lightly to coat.

4. Tip the salad onto a large serving platter and coarsely grate over the remaining Parmesan, then drizzle over the remaining dressing and serve.

TOP TIP

This is a great one to make for a quick, solo dinner, with leftovers for a workday lunch the next day.

BLACK BEAN, SWEET POTATO + TENDERSTEM BROCCOLI BOWLS

Feeds 3–4
Takes 50 minutes

This is one to get your gut microbes partying. We all know beans are GREAT for our gut health, thanks to their high fibre content. But here we've introduced a creamy miso kefir dressing full of prebiotics, which feed the good bacteria in our guts. The seed topper adds crunch, but also packs in a few more plant points to make this dish sing.

---

4 sweet potatoes, chopped into bite-sized chunks

2 red onions, each cut into 8

3 tbsp olive oil

1 tsp cayenne pepper or hot paprika

1 tsp maple syrup

200g (7oz) Tenderstem broccoli / 1 head of broccoli, broken into florets and stalk roughly chopped

570g (1lb 4½oz) jarred black beans, drained and rinsed

few big handfuls of spinach (or use a mixed watercress, spinach and rocket salad bag)

handful of coriander, finely chopped

salt and pepper

FOR THE SUPER-SEED SPRINKLE

200g (7oz) mixed seeds, such as sunflower seeds, pumpkin seeds, sesame seeds and linseeds

1 tbsp olive oil

½ tsp cayenne or chilli powder

1 tsp honey or maple syrup

FOR THE DRESSING

100ml (3½fl oz) kefir

2 tsp white miso paste

1 tbsp tahini

1 small garlic clove, finely grated

½ tsp maple syrup or honey

juice of ½ lime / ½ tbsp rice vinegar

1. Preheat the oven to 180°C/160°C fan/350°F/gas mark 4 and line a baking tray with baking paper.

2. To make the super-seed sprinkle, mix all the ingredients together in a bowl and spread onto the prepared tray. Roast for 10–15 minutes until dry and golden, stirring once during cooking. Keep an eye on it, as the seeds easily burn! Allow to cool and store in a sealed container.

3. With the oven still on, spread out the sweet potato and onions in an even layer on a baking tray and toss well with 2 tablespoons of the olive oil, the cayenne pepper or paprika, and a pinch of salt and pepper. Roast for 25 minutes.

4. Remove the sweet potatoes from the oven and drizzle with the maple syrup, giving the potatoes a turn in the tray. Add the broccoli to the tray and drizzle with the remaining olive oil. Sprinkle with salt and roast everything for a further 15 minutes, or until the broccoli is slightly charred and the sweet potatoes are soft and tender.

5. Meanwhile, in a small bowl, whisk together all the dressing ingredients until well combined. Season to taste.

6. Once cooked, remove the veg from the oven and tip the black beans onto the tray. Toss gently to combine with the oils and spices. If you like having a warm salad, you can serve straight away with the cooling dressing. Or you can leave the veggies to cool and serve it cold.

7. To assemble, tumble the veg and beans, along with a few handfuls of spinach or salad leaves, onto a serving platter. Drizzle over some of the dressing, leaving the rest to serve on the side. Garnish with chopped coriander and a few spoonfuls of the seed topper.

TOP TIP

If you can't find kefir, use the same amount of natural yoghurt instead. This recipe makes a big batch of the super-seed sprinkle, which you can store in a jar for up to 3 weeks.

THANK YOUS

They say it takes a village to raise a child — well, this book is our second-born, and it's been lovingly raised by a full-blown community of bean-obsessives.

The Bold Bean team has doubled in size (!) since our first book — and I know that by the time this book enters the world, there will be even more of you. The whole team is part of making this a success — thank you.

A huge shout-out to Jess, who masterfully managed our community contributor recipes, orchestrating endless back-and-forths, collating feedback, and making sure the final versions were as knock-out as the rest of the recipes in the book.

To Martha, who worked so closely with Juliette to ensure this book feels innately, unapologetically Bold Bean — your commitment to our brand identity is all over these pages.

To Sophie Godwin, for your sharp editorial eye and care, and to Esther Clark, for all the idea-sparking that made our creative gears charge into action. To Cat Sarsfield, for the stunning copy that brings our recipes to life. To Jo, Juliette, and the whole team at Kyle Books and Octopus, who took a bet on us with Bold Beans and again with this book. We hope this one, like the first, makes you proud to have taken the bet on a little bean business with a big mission!

To Alejandra, who analyzed our beans to show JUST how healthy they are.

To Nancy, our unstoppable publicist, whose tireless efforts helped make Bold Beans the success we needed to be here again with *Full of Beans*.

To Sam Harris, our phenomenal photographer, and Kitty Coles, our styling whizz — your work has made this book as beautiful as it is delicious. And, of course, Emily Sweet, for seeing something in us years ago and continuing to bring us wins.

To Hannah, once again at the creative helm of recipe creation. Your talent is bringing joy, beauty and deliciousness to beans, and everything you touch turns into something I want to eat.

To our Bean Buds — our secret weapon. This book would be far less tasty without your honest critiques, recipe testing and enthusiastic feedback. You brought clarity to the chaos, tested our limits (and our patience), and made sure these recipes are truly foolproof. You are the soul of this cookbook, and we can't thank you enough.

To Kelly MacKenzie and Shabanna Brown from White Bear Studio who helped us bring the look and feel of our new Bold Bean packaging into this book.

Finally, thank you to every single person who bought a copy of *Bold Beans* and made it a runaway success. Without you — your love, your cooking, your word-of-mouth enthusiasm — this second book wouldn't exist. You are our BEAN CHAMPS, and this book is yours as much as it is ours.

RECIPE CONTRIBUTORS

Xuxa Milrose
Raina Patel
Stephen Blades
Mark Whenman
Sarah Liveing
Samantha Leung
Rhia Patel
Catherine Sarsfield
Jasvinder Kaur
Sheel Patel
Mónica Alazraki
Fred Leeming
Jane Hart
Susie Flory
Rinku Dutt
Susanna Bowers

RECIPE TESTERS

Hester Rowell
Ralph Lee
Jane Stedman
Stephanie Pettigrew
Clare Hughes
Natali Shatchan
Anna Sawicki Smith
Ben Jacobs
Jo Duffield
Laura Endicott
Fiona Watson
Karen Richard
Carol White
Deborah Loftus
Nick and Sophie Dodd
Rebecca Ward
Anna Harris-Noble
Jo Irwin
Sophie Myers
David Malakoty
Lucy Redmore
Patricia Farrelly
Steph Weiss
Olivia Rosenvinge
Tereza Ward
Robin Gill
Linda Brosnan
Sarah Cudmore
Fay Haworth
Philippa Mann
Liz Foster
Stephanie Blake
Serina Tatham
Patricia Hatton
Chris Sumsion
Huw Purssell
Beth Liley
Francesca O'Keeffe
Hannah Owen
Lucy Sandys-Clarke
Rachel Besenyei
Charlotte Humphery
Ellie Lundberg
Sophie Izard
Rachel Hardy
Alison Walton
Katie Pitcher
Edward Bartkowiak
Molly Martin
Anastasia Nicholl-Pierson
Hayley Alton
Eilidh Matheson
Francesca Byrne
Lydia D'Souza
Hannah McGregor
Amber Mounsey
Laura Negus
Charlotte Araya Moreland
Lauren Blackhall
Bella Boxall
Alexia Seabrook
Maia White
Hermione Banks
Anna de Winton
Lauren Walker
Anna Fitzgerald
Patrick Martin
Georgia Billings
Emma Jones
Kate Cardinal
Shaquira Jeyasingh
Ruth Brent
Harriet Makin
Alice Chissell
Imogen Birkett
Nicola Sleat
Carey Allen
Maia White
Lisa Mortimer
Paula Ridge
Cerys Seys Llewellyn
Ying Tan
Isabelle Whittle
Janine Monk
Charlie Raines
Ellie Walton
Sue Hall
Jasmin Jilma
Maggie Day
Dawn Spence
Richard Williams
Deirdre Healy
Grace Huxford
Helen Todd
Minnie Watson
Octavia Warren
Catherine Webb
Daisy Blacker
Jacqui Wills
Anna Wilson
Rebecca Bray
Grace McAleer-Ryder
Maddy Delaney
Susannah Deane
Amy McWilliams
Elspeth Langsdale
Holly Ransley
Morven Millar
Lani Girard
Sophie Hanson
Sara Williams
Elysia Garland
Cormac Kennedy
Aaron Labaton
Todd Harris
Philippa Kneeshaw
Guy Whitehead
Lissy Garland
Poppy Tuckley
Jenny Cudmore
Phoebe Cardew
Stephanie Weiss
Felicity Kneeshaw
Ellie Daynes
Liv Hastie
Emily Greenberg
Susie Liddell
Kate Haworth
Kitty Grubb
Elspeth E. Langsdale
William Wells
Jane Johnson
Anna Tingle
Lauren Froese
Sarah Hubbard
Mhairi Millar
Jasmin Jilma

BOLD BEAN TEAM

Amelia Christie-Miller
Edward Whelpton
Hannah Wilding
Martha Jensen
Lucy Bridge
Rosa Hernandez
Jess Beddoe
Louisa Sorensen
Charlie Hanks
Clara Moro
Nakira Bozickovic
Lucy Cowan
Kate Voss
James Robinson
Fiona Cramp
Lucy Barks
Alejandra Garcia
Issie Mosley
Beth Latham
Alex Haldane

COOKBOOK TEAM

Joanna Copestick
Juliette Norsworthy
Nicky Collings
Sarah Reece
Sam A Harris
Kitty Coles
Sophie Godwin
Emily Sweet
Tara O'Sullivan
Allison Gonsalves

THANK YOUS

INDEX

aglio e olio beans 137
aji verde greens + white beans 67
anchovies: cherry tomato, anchovy + white bean gratin 158
asparagus
    spring green beanotto 151
    watercress + white bean soup with charred asparagus 143
aubergines
    borlotti *alla Norma* with creamy ricotta 72
    curried chickpeas + aubergine 66
avocado
    borlotti bean fajitas with zesty avocado cream 82
    cheesy bean quesadillas 165
    miso black beans with chicken + lime 65

bacon
    cheesy bean brunch hotcakes with maple bacon 121
    queen chickpea BLT salad 61
baked beans 162–5
    cheesy bean quesadillas 165
    Med-veg, black olive + feta bake 164
    pasta alla guanciale 163
beanottos 40–3, 151, 152
    beetroot + goats' cheese 40
    butternut squash + sage 42
    chorizo + cherry tomato 43
    creamy courgette 41
    porcini mushroom 152
    spring green 151
beef + black bean picadillo bake with sweet potatoes + creole salsa 176–7
beetroot
    beetroot + goats' cheese beanotto 40
    beetroot + borlotti beans 64
    beetroot, red bean + mackerel salad 132
    black bean, beetroot + walnut dip 180
black beans 166
    beef + black bean picadillo bake with sweet potatoes + creole salsa 176–7
    black bean, beetroot + walnut dip 180
    black bean makhani with kachumber salad 175
    black bean-stuffed pepper feast with yoghurt + a pomegranate salad 181
    black bean, sweet potato + tenderstem broccoli bowls 186
    cold sesame black bean noodles 170
    garlicky za'atar black beans + tomatoes 112
    miso black beans with chicken + lime 65
    punchy peanut, ginger + black bean curry with buttered wild rice 172
    seeded caper, shallot + Parmesan black bean salad 185
    spicy bean paratha pockets 178
    sweetcorn + black bean fritters with tomato + red onion salsa 169
borlotti beans 68
    beetroot + borlotti beans 64
    borlotti *alla Norma* with creamy ricotta 72
    borlotti bean fajitas with zesty avocado cream 82
    borlotti beans *con le sarde* 70
    cacio e pepe borlotti beans 75
    fresh pesto borlottis with chargrilled courgettes + tomatoes 83
    sausage, broccoli + pecorino beans 78
    sausage meatballs with borlotti beans, fennel + mozzarella 76–7
    speedy tuna + borlotti bean salad 86
    spiced onion + borlotti bean frittata 81
broccoli
    aglio e olio beans 137
    aji verde greens + white beans 67
    black bean, sweet potato + tenderstem broccoli bowls 186
    cold sesame black bean noodles 170
    romesco sauce with crispy butter beans + capers 20
    sausage, broccoli + pecorino beans 78
brown butter + caper beans with raw courgette salad 39
butter beans 12
    beany cauliflower cheese with sherry cherry tomatoes 23
    brown butter + caper beans with raw courgette salad 39
    butter bean saganaki 19
    butter bean tagine feast with olive + lemon salsa 31
    caramelised fennel, sun-dried tomato + butter bean salad 37
    cheesy Marmite butter beans on toast with pickled shallots 16
    creamy coconut + tomato curry 24
    creamy leek, mushroom + butter bean pie 28
    curried cauliflower + butter bean flatbreads 88
    lemony ricotta + butter bean dip with smashed crispy potatoes 30
    romesco sauce with crispy butter beans + capers 20
    sausage + butter bean stew 27
    tomato soup with cheesy butter beans 14
    za'atar butter bean salad with creamy butter bean dip 35
butternut squash *see* squash

***cacio* e pepe** borlotti beans 75
Cajun-spiced chickpeas + rice 88
cannellini beans *see* white beans
capers
    brown butter + caper beans with raw courgette salad 39
    romesco sauce with crispy butter beans + capers 20
    seeded caper, shallot + Parmesan black bean salad 185
    tonnato beans with tomatoes + capers 146
    white beans + charred cabbage with caper + parsley vinaigrette 149
caramelised fennel, sun-dried tomato + butter bean salad 37
carlin peas 90
    carlin pea caprese 102
    carlin pea chaat 96
    carlin pea ploughman's salad 107
    carlin pea saag with mango chutney-glazed halloumi 98
    carlin pea stroganoff 101
    crispy baked halloumi, carlin pea + orange salad 108
    double pea toasts with pea smash, feta + crispy carlin peas 92
    fish finger + curried carlin pea sandos 95
    roasted squash with creamy Marmite carlins + crispy sage 103
carrots: one-pan chickpea, roasted grape + caramelised carrot with baked feta 62
cauliflower
    beany cauliflower cheese with sherry cherry tomatoes 23
    crunchy chickpeas, spicy cauliflower, whipped feta + pomegranate slaw 52–3
    curried cauliflower + butter bean flatbreads 88
cheese
    aji verde greens + white beans 67
    beany cauliflower cheese with sherry cherry tomatoes 23
    beetroot + goats' cheese beanotto 40
    beetroot + borlotti beans 64
    borlotti *alla Norma* with creamy ricotta 72
    butter bean saganaki 19
    cacio e pepe borlotti beans 75
    caramelised fennel, sun-dried tomato + butter bean salad 37
    carlin pea caprese 102
    carlin pea ploughman's salad 107
    carlin pea saag with mango chutney-glazed halloumi 98
    cheesy bean brunch hotcakes with maple bacon 121
    cheesy bean quesadillas 165
    cheesy Marmite butter beans on toast with pickled shallots 16
    chipotle red kidney beans + baked feta 111
    chunky feta yoghurt, sun-ripened tomatoes + chickpeas with focaccia 51
    creamy courgette beanotto 41
    creamy pea pesto 135
    crispy baked halloumi, carlin pea + orange salad 108
    crunchy chickpeas, spicy cauliflower, whipped feta + pomegranate slaw 52–3
    double pea toasts with pea smash, feta + crispy carlin peas 92
    lemony ricotta + butter bean dip with smashed crispy potatoes 30
    Med-veg, black olive + feta bake 164
    Mexican-inspired bean salad with crispy tortilla croutons 161
    mushroom ragu + cheesy bean béchamel lasagne 156–7
    'nduja beans, mozzarella + hot honey 122
    one-pan chickpea, roasted grape + caramelised carrot with baked feta 62
    rajma kebabs with lettuce cups, raita + cumin potatoes 116–17
    roasted squash with creamy Marmite carlins + crispy sage 103
    sausage, broccoli + pecorino beans 78
    sausage meatballs with borlotti beans, fennel + mozzarella 76–7
    seeded caper, shallot + Parmesan black bean salad 185
    spiced onion + borlotti bean frittata 81
    tomato + mascarpone 135
    tomato soup with cheesy butter beans 14
    whipped red beans + crispy rice salad 131
cherry tomato, anchovy + white bean gratin 158
chicken
    cosy chicken + white bean soup with crispy chicken-skin croutons 140
    fresh pesto borlottis with chargrilled courgettes + tomatoes 83
    miso black beans with chicken + lime 65
    peri peri chicken + lemony beans 155
chickpeas 44
    Cajun-spiced chickpeas + rice 88
    chickpea, sweet potato + peanut butter curry 57
    chickpea, tomato + harissa stew with herby yoghurt 58
    chunky feta yoghurt, sun-ripened tomatoes + chickpeas with focaccia 51
    crunchy chickpeas, spicy cauliflower, whipped feta + pomegranate slaw 52–3
    curried chickpeas + aubergine 66
    curried chickpeas + paneer 113
    one-pan chickpea, roasted grape + caramelised carrot with baked feta 62

pickled cucumber with chickpeas +
    sticky rice 48
queen chickpea BLT salad 61
silky roasted garlic hummus +
    courgette bowl 46
smashed chickpeas on toast with fried
    egg + pickled cucumbers 54
chipotle red kidney beans + baked feta 111
chorizo
    chorizo + cherry tomato beanotto 43
    crispy chorizo + red bean shakshuka
        with charred padron peppers 119
    Mediterranean cod, chorizo + red bean
        stew 128
cod
    harissa cod + white beans 110
    Mediterranean cod, chorizo + red bean
        stew 128
courgettes
    aji verde greens + white beans 67
    brown butter + caper beans with raw
        courgette salad 39
    creamy courgette beanotto 41
    fresh pesto borlottis with chargrilled
        courgettes + tomatoes 83
    silky roasted garlic hummus +
        courgette bowl 46
cucumber
    black bean makhani with kachumber
        salad 175
    curried chickpeas + aubergine 66
    pickled cucumber with chickpeas +
        sticky rice 48
    rajma kebabs with lettuce cups, raita +
        cumin potatoes 116–17
    smashed chickpeas on toast with fried
        egg + pickled cucumbers 54
    za'atar butter bean salad with creamy
        butter bean dip 35
curries
    chickpea, sweet potato + peanut butter
        curry 57
    creamy coconut + tomato curry 24
    curried cauliflower + butter bean
        flatbreads 88
    curried chickpeas + aubergine 66
    curried chickpeas + paneer 113
    fish finger + curried carlin pea sandos 95
    punchy peanut, ginger + black bean
        curry with buttered wild rice 172

eggs
    crispy white beans + sage-fried eggs
        with garlicky greens 144
    smashed chickpeas on toast with fried
        egg + pickled cucumbers 54
    spiced onion + borlotti bean frittata 81

fennel
    borlotti beans con le sarde 70
    caramelised fennel, sun-dried tomato +
        butter bean salad 37
    creamy sausage + fennel 136
    sausage meatballs with borlotti beans,
        fennel + mozzarella 76–7
fish finger + curried carlin pea sandos 95

garlic
    crispy white beans + sage-fried eggs
        with garlicky greens 144
    garlicky za'atar black beans + tomatoes 112
    silky roasted garlic hummus +
        courgette bowl 46

harissa
    chickpea, tomato + harissa stew with
        herby yoghurt 58
    harissa cod + white beans 110

leeks: creamy leek, mushroom + butter bean
    pie 28
lemons
    butter bean tagine feast with olive +
        lemon salsa 31
    lemony ricotta + butter bean dip with
        smashed crispy potatoes 30
lettuce
    aji verde greens + white beans 67
    queen chickpea BLT salad 61
    rajma kebabs with lettuce cups, raita +
        cumin potatoes 116–17

mackerel: beetroot, red bean + mackerel
    salad 132
Med-veg, black olive + feta bake 164
Mediterranean cod, chorizo + red bean
    stew 128
Mexican-inspired bean salad with crispy
    tortilla croutons 161
miso black beans with chicken + lime 65
mushrooms
    carlin pea stroganoff 101
    creamy leek, mushroom + butter bean
        pie 28
    mushroom ragu + cheesy bean
        béchamel lasagne 156–7
    porcini mushroom beanotto 152

'nduja beans, mozzarella + hot honey 122
noodles: cold sesame black bean noodles 170

olives
    butter bean tagine feast with olive +
        lemon salsa 31
    Med-veg, black olive + feta bake 164
one-pan chickpea, roasted grape +
    caramelised carrot with baked feta 62
oranges: crispy baked halloumi, carlin pea +
    orange salad 108

pancetta: creamy leek, mushroom + butter
    bean pie 28
paneer: curried chickpeas + paneer 113
pasta *alla guanciale* 163
peanut butter
    chickpea, sweet potato + peanut butter
        curry 57
    punchy peanut, ginger + black bean
        curry with buttered wild rice 172
peas
    creamy pea pesto 135
    double pea toasts with pea smash, feta
        + crispy carlin peas 92
    spring green beanotto 151
peppers
    black bean-stuffed pepper feast with
        yoghurt + a pomegranate salad 181
    borlotti bean fajitas with zesty avocado
        cream 82
    crispy chorizo + red bean shakshuka
        with charred padron peppers 119
    Med-veg, black olive + feta bake 164
    romesco sauce with crispy butter beans
        + capers 20
peri peri chicken + lemony beans 155
pesto
    creamy pea pesto 135
    fresh pesto borlottis with chargrilled
        courgettes + tomatoes 83
    spring green beanotto 151
pomegranate
    black bean-stuffed pepper feast with
        yoghurt + a pomegranate salad 181
    crunchy chickpeas, spicy cauliflower,
        whipped feta + pomegranate slaw
        52–3
porcini mushroom beanotto 152

prawns: butter bean saganaki 19

rajma kebabs with lettuce cups, raita +
    cumin potatoes 116–17
red kidney beans 114
    beetroot, red bean + mackerel salad 132
    cheesy bean brunch hotcakes with
        maple bacon 121
    chipotle red kidney beans + baked feta 111
    crispy chorizo + red bean shakshuka
        with charred padron peppers 119
    Mediterranean cod, chorizo + red bean
        stew 128
    'nduja beans, mozzarella + hot honey 122
    rajma kebabs with lettuce cups, raita +
        cumin potatoes 116–17
    smoky chilli with fluffy sweetcorn
        dumplings 124
    smoky kimchi beans with crispy tempeh
        crumb 127
    whipped red beans + crispy rice salad 131
rice
    Cajun-spiced chickpeas + rice 88
    pickled cucumber with chickpeas +
        sticky rice 48
    punchy peanut, ginger + black bean
        curry with buttered wild rice 172
    whipped red beans + crispy rice salad 131
romesco sauce with crispy butter beans +
    capers 20

sage
    butternut squash + sage beanotto 42
    roasted squash with creamy Marmite
        carlins + crispy sage 103
salads
    aji verde greens + white beans 67
    beetroot + borlotti beans 64
    beetroot, red bean + mackerel salad 132
    brown butter + caper beans with raw
        courgette salad 39
    carlin pea ploughman's salad 107
    crispy baked halloumi, carlin pea +
        orange salad 108
    curried chickpeas + aubergine 66
    fresh pesto borlottis with chargrilled
        courgettes + tomatoes 83
    Mexican-inspired bean salad with crispy
        tortilla croutons 161
    miso black beans with chicken + lime 65
    queen chickpea BLT salad 61
    speedy tuna + borlotti bean salad 86
    whipped red beans + crispy rice salad 131
    za'atar butter bean salad with creamy
        butter bean dip 35
salsa
    beef + black bean picadillo bake with
        sweet potatoes + creole salsa 176–7
    butter bean tagine feast with olive +
        lemon salsa 31
    sausage + butter bean stew 27
    sweetcorn + black bean fritters with
        tomato + red onion salsa 169
sardines: borlotti beans *con le sarde* 70
sauces
    aglio e olio beans 137
    creamy pea pesto 135
    creamy sausage + fennel 136
    tomato + mascarpone 135
sausages
    creamy sausage + fennel 136
    sausage, broccoli + pecorino beans 78
    sausage + butter bean stew 27
    sausage meatballs with borlotti beans,
        fennel + mozzarella 76–7
soup
    cosy chicken + white bean soup with
        crispy chicken-skin croutons 140

tomato soup with cheesy butter beans 14
watercress + white bean soup with charred asparagus 143

spinach
  beetroot + borlotti beans 64
  black bean, sweet potato + tenderstem broccoli bowls 186
  carlin pea saag with mango chutney-glazed halloumi 98
  chickpea, sweet potato + peanut butter curry 57
  creamy coconut + tomato curry 24
  smoky kimchi beans with crispy tempeh crumb 127
  spring green beanotto 151
spring green beanotto 151
squash
  butternut squash + sage beanotto 42
  roasted squash with creamy Marmite carlins + crispy sage 103
stews
  chickpea, tomato + harissa stew with herby yoghurt 58
  Mediterranean cod, chorizo + red bean stew 128
  sausage + butter bean stew 27
sweet potatoes
  beef + black bean picadillo bake with sweet potatoes + creole salsa 176–7
  black bean, sweet potato + tenderstem broccoli bowls 186
  chickpea, sweet potato + peanut butter curry 57
sweetcorn
  smoky chilli with fluffy sweetcorn dumplings 124
  sweetcorn + black bean fritters with tomato + red onion salsa 169

tempeh: smoky kimchi beans with crispy tempeh crumb 127
tomatoes
  beany cauliflower cheese with sherry cherry tomatoes 23

black bean makhani with kachumber salad 175
borlotti *alla Norma* with creamy ricotta 72
borlotti bean fajitas with zesty avocado cream 82
butter bean saganaki 19
caramelised fennel, sun-dried tomato + butter bean salad 37
carlin pea caprese 102
cherry tomato, anchovy + white bean gratin 158
chickpea, tomato + harissa stew with herby yoghurt 58
chorizo + cherry tomato beanotto 43
chunky feta yoghurt, sun-ripened tomatoes + chickpeas with focaccia 51
creamy coconut + tomato curry 24
crispy chorizo + red bean shakshuka with charred padron peppers 119
curried chickpeas + aubergine 66
fresh pesto borlottis with chargrilled courgettes + tomatoes 83
garlicky za'atar black beans + tomatoes 112
Mexican-inspired bean salad with crispy tortilla croutons 161
queen chickpea BLT salad 61
sausage + butter bean stew 27
smoky chilli with fluffy sweetcorn dumplings 124
sweetcorn + black bean fritters with tomato + red onion salsa 169
tomato + mascarpone 135
tomato soup with cheesy butter beans 14
tonnato beans with tomatoes + capers 146
traybakes 110–13
tuna
  speedy tuna + borlotti bean salad 86
  tonnato beans with tomatoes + capers 146

walnuts: black bean, beetroot + walnut dip 180

watercress + white bean soup with charred asparagus 143
whipped red beans + crispy rice salad 131
white beans 138
  aji verde greens + white beans 67
  beetroot + goats' cheese beanotto 40
  butternut squash + sage beanotto 42
  cherry tomato, anchovy + white bean gratin 158
  chorizo + cherry tomato beanotto 43
  cosy chicken + white bean soup with crispy chicken-skin croutons 140
  creamy courgette beanotto 41
  crispy white beans + sage-fried eggs with garlicky greens 144
  harissa cod + white beans 110
  Mexican-inspired bean salad with crispy tortilla croutons 161
  mushroom ragu + cheesy bean béchamel lasagne 156–7
  peri peri chicken + lemony beans 155
  porcini mushroom beanotto 152
  spring green beanotto 151
  tonnato beans with tomatoes + capers 146
  watercress + white bean soup with charred asparagus 143
  white beans + charred cabbage with caper + parsley vinaigrette 149

yoghurt
  black bean-stuffed pepper feast with yoghurt + a pomegranate salad 181
  chickpea, tomato + harissa stew with herby yoghurt 58
  chunky feta yoghurt, sun-ripened tomatoes + chickpeas with focaccia 51

za'atar
  garlicky za'atar black beans + tomatoes 112
  za'atar butter bean salad with creamy butter bean dip 35

GLOSSARY

INGREDIENTS

Aubergine – eggplant
Beetroot – beets
Bicarbonate of soda – baking soda
Caster sugar – superfine sugar
Chicory – endive
Coriander (fresh) – cilantro
Cornflour – cornstarch
Courgette – zucchini
Double cream – heavy cream
Mangetout – snow peas
Natural yoghurt – plain yogurt
Peppers (red/green/yellow) – bell peppers
Plain flour – all-purpose flour
Rapeseed oil – canola oil
Rocket – arugula
Soured cream – sour cream
Spring onions – scallions
Stock – broth
Sultanas – golden raisins
Tenderstem broccoli – broccolini
Tomato purée – tomato paste

EQUIPMENT

Baking paper – parchment paper
Griddle pan – grill pan
Grill – broiler
Roasting tray – roasting pan
Sieve – fine mesh strainer

PICTURE CREDITS

Page 10: Hodmedods.co.uk; iStock/ AlasdairJames, boommaval boommaval, chengyuzheng, ClaudioVentrella, ECummings00, Everyday better to do everything you love, IMAG35, Inna Tarasenko, Karimitsu, Marilyna, maxsol7, PicturePartners, Popovaphoto, SIAATH, tfazevedo, Vergani_Fotografia, xamtiw
Page 12: © 2024 Jamie Oliver Enterprises Ltd, photography Richard Clatworthy
Page 40: iStock Antonio Gravante, PotaeRin

Page 68: Bree Dunbar
Page 114: Angela Catlin
Page 138: Ola O. Smit
Page 166: Max Miechowski